UNDER PRESSURE

BURIED ALIVE AND OTHER ORDINARY MIRACLES

By Paul Joseph Brennan

Love you
Love you work
Sincerely
Paul Joseph Brennan

Rah dsrael!

Red Mountain Shadows Publishing
Cover Design by Serena Clarke
Printed in the United States of America

Under Pressure: Buried Alive and Other Ordinary Miracles
By Paul Joseph Brennan

ISBN-13: 978-1981218882

ISBN-10: 1981218882

Dedication

This book is dedicated to my mother. She chose self-improvement over self-indulgence. She worked her way through nursing school while having to raise and feed five of us. She walked to school then work, waited on tables, and walked home again. Mary Brennan was diligent. She did whatever it took. She never gave up on me! She always saw the good. When I get tired or knocked down, I think of Mom B and I get up again. I miss you, Mom! (Chumbawamba!)

Table of Contents

Prologue

They say your life flashes before your eyes when you are about to leave this planet. I happen to know that is true because I found myself in a heap of trouble on this particular day. And I mean a heap! How I got myself into this predicament is pretty clear looking back, but who knew that my life was about to end so suddenly and so traumatically? This couldn't be happening. Am I really going to die this way? Smothered to death with no air and no room to breathe in even if I had air?

Wait God! I am a good guy, a good son, a good husband, a good father. Why me? Why now? No! This is NOT OK! I can get myself out of this because I have enough faith to move mountains. I need to move this mountain of dirt off the top of me, so I can climb out of this trench. This intense crushing is unbearable... This is insane...

The day started out as a pretty normal day... as far as days go. I was quite frustrated that I wasn't where I really wanted to be in life. It felt like I was at a dead end in my career. It was frustrating, and I felt "stuck" to try whatever I could to provide for my family, because there were limited job opportunities. My friend, Jody, and I had been discussing it for the past few days. All either one of us really wanted to do was to be able to give lectures and classes, teaching people about health and how to keep their bodies and minds functioning properly.

As it was, we were stuck digging sewer lines!

It was mandatory for all the houses to switch from septic tanks to sewer lines, but neither Jody nor I could afford to pay anyone to do this for us, so we were doing it ourselves with a backhoe. We figured that as long as we had to rent the backhoe, we might as well do this for a few of our neighbors to make back the money we paid to rent the machine and maybe even make a little cash as well. This would also save our neighbors more than half of the normal cost to hire someone else to do it.

Though I was thankful for the money this provided, we were still frustrated that we had to do this instead of following our dreams. I kept saying how I felt "trapped" and hated what we had to do to make money. Little did I know that I was going to literally be "trapped" just a few short moments later. Are our words really that strong that we can cause things to happen just by saying something out loud? I always felt that it was important to keep my words on the positive side, but I was about to find out just how important that was.

I had been at the hospital with my 14-year-old daughter, as she had been admitted for surgery to remove her appendix. I left the job to Jody, but I was feeling a little nervous, because I knew that the hole we'd dug was not shored up very secure and I knew the dirt wasn't very stable. I wanted to be there to help make sure we could get the sewer pipe in and glued and get that hole backfilled as soon as possible. I had even told my wife that I needed to get back to work as quick as I could.

Well, my daughter's surgery went fine and she came home that afternoon. Now, the matter at hand was to finish this job and get on with the next one.

The owner of the home we were working on had cut his sprinkler line and forgotten to shut off the system, so the hole had filled completely with water and mud. The next morning, we came upon a muddy pond.

I had to use the bucket of the backhoe to dip the water out.

I only needed to be in the trench for a few seconds... Yet here I was, trapped beneath 8-10 feet of muddy, wet, heavy earth.

First, before I move on, let's get to my life that brought me to this point... Things that I feel are important enough to make public because of how each of those events or times caused me to become who I am today, as well as some of the things I've learned along the way. I am in no way trying to say that I am any more special than anyone else or that I'm any smarter than anyone else. On the contrary. But I do know who I am, as far as being a son of a Heavenly Father who loves me and who has, for whatever reason, given me many miracles to keep me alive and has helped me get to this point in my life.

I also know that I am not unique in this aspect either. He is there for each one of us! We are all on an individual journey and it's up to each one of us to recognize our own miracles and blessings. As you read, you'll also realize that I'm not afraid to ask for miracles. God wants to bless us, but He won't force himself on us. It's up to us to open that door.

I'm assuming you realize that I made it out of that trench, since I'm here now writing this story, but you'll have to keep reading for the details. I think you'll find they are worth the read. Each chapter in this book is a separate story of parts of my life. They are all completely true. However, names have been changed to protect the "guilty" and the innocent. These stories have all molded me into who I have become. They are all "ordinary miracles" ... as ordinary as the air we breathe. You'll understand what I mean by this later. Of course, I am being facetious, as miracles are amazing and none are ordinary.

We all have miracles in our lives. Do we recognize them for what they are or do we chalk them up to coincidences? As I tell my story, remember this is life flashing-before-your-eyes mode, laying beneath the crushing earth, but in slow-mo... Here goes!

Chapter 1

Boston Children's Hospital

This is the story of Paul. This first chapter explains in part why I am the way I am. I don't apologize. I am "me" because of my beginnings and I am a product of my past. We all have a past, a present and a future. It's not where we were yesterday that counts, but what we do with today and who we are trying to become tomorrow! I am certainly not perfect, as you will clearly see.

My parents-
Gene R. Brennan and Mary Jane Hanley. Married 3 times just to get it right…

I'll tell you about the first two right now. The third one will be later on in the book. You see, Mary Jane, a devout Catholic knew there was no other Holy Matrimony than being married in the Catholic Church. Gene, on the other hand, born out of wedlock, was raised by his grandmother then eventually turned over to a foster family. I can't really remember the details, but I am a prodigy of fetal alcohol syndrome.

So as ADHD, ADD, and Dyslexia plays on a guy—you could probably read this book backwards and catch a better vision. Like I said, no apologies! I am who I am and I do jump around a bit, but I will try to help you follow my journey as best as I can.

My dad's foster brother was a Protestant minister as well as an attorney. He married the two of them, but of course mom could not live without the blessings of the Catholic Church, so they got married again, this time by a Catholic priest. It still made no difference. They were heading for divorce and they just didn't know they were on the "broken family tour bus." It was like the scenic route, but they finally divorced years later. Just think of all the fights they would've missed out on if they had done it sooner.

Dad was a bartender and allowed mom one drink only while she was pregnant with me. Well, mom must have thought it was one drink from each one of their friends and they had a lot of friends! And they all thought it was pretty funny that Mary could drink everybody under the table and not even show signs of getting drunk.

Well if she, in her pregnant state, was staying sober, do you wonder who might have been the one getting drunk? By the way, I look up to all my siblings, literally. They're all taller than me. Now that pisses me off! Does this have something to do with all that alcohol?

Combine this start in life with all the later head injuries, three broken collarbones, 16 stitches in the skull, falling 12 feet onto my head and stopping by a concrete basement apartment when I was two, falling on a picket fence, and 16 more stitches, this time opposite my head very close to my *ass*-ett, which almost made me sterile.

In my formative years, I was bitten by eight dogs, two of which were Doberman Pinschers. I was the only white boy in that yard among thirty other children. These dogs had never seen a white boy before, so I guess you couldn't blame them! I must have tasted like chicken. And they must have spread the word to get a piece of this guy because six more came at me at different times...all different sizes...all in that same neighborhood. They all traveled in packs from "the projects".

My mom told me that when I was just a few years old a pack of these wild dogs encircled me while she looked out the side window of our apartment building. Her blood ran chill and there was no way to warn me, as the slightest movement would have caused them to tear me apart like a rag-doll. All she could do was pray. Thankfully, that prayer was answered. I can't remember the details, but I do remember I was wearing my cowboy hat, six shooter cap gun and fake cowhide chaps. I don't even remember that circle of dogs, but I do remember how it felt when eight other dogs bit me at different times, all breaking through my skin.

Believe it or not, I am a dog lover! Our first dog was a female boxer. She was so wonderful and protective, and she took good care of us. She would go and get the newspaper from the corner grocery store and pay for it with the money placed in her leather collar, and heaven help you if you tried to get the money and were not the owner of the drugstore.

From toddler to seven-years old, we called the projects "home". The projects were a low-income neighborhood filled to the brim with the lowest of the low. Dirt, drugs, crime. All in a world of stacked apartment buildings, scary alleyways, and squalor. There were good people there too, in the midst of all of this, but they were harder to find. One sweet elderly black lady, named Miss Teddy, encouraged my mother to get my sister out of this neighborhood. She was concerned it would only bring my sister trouble by remaining in that area. Especially being a white family in a mostly black neighborhood in the '60s.

Back to dad... remember, he was turned over to foster care as a boy. Being the oldest of 13 foster children in the foster-care system, he had to turn all his money over to the home. He also endured daily beatings, to the point where if they skipped a day he wondered what was wrong. He grew up and became a hard worker and tried to make a life with what he had, but needless to say, he grew up with a chip on his shoulder. While he had to endure a miserable upbringing, his sired father was a millionaire playboy whose parents refused to let him take the responsibility of his actions.

My father did the best he could at the time with the hand he was dealt. In fact, he joined the military at an early age and became feared and respected. In his days in the military, during World War II, he was a corporal by the end of that war. Nobody got advancements, but my dad got his.

My father also had a sense of decency. He hated to see men use power and violence against others. Perhaps because he had been a product of it himself. I remember once my dad saw three men beating on this old neighborhood drunk in front of our house in Roxbury. For the first few minutes of the fight it was somewhat even because my mother had a hold of my dad's arm, trying to hold him back. She kept begging him not to fight. Yeah right!

When he broke free of her, he picked one of the guys up over his head and slammed him on the curb, breaking his back. It ended the fight, but my mom was just as pissed off at him as he was at the three men. I don't know who was crazier in my family, my mom or my dad, but I got a lot of both of them flowing in my veins. I had a very hot Irish temper cursed from both sides of the family. I did not need alcohol; I just needed an excuse, leaning on the verge of bipolar. By the way, the telling of these stories will remain G rated as I have grandkids now that will read this, but you've got to realize the language in my house was very close to what prison language is like or a bunch of drunk sailors.

While I'm on the topic of prison language…

My business associate, Roger, was building a spec home in a very prestigious neighborhood and stopped by in his business suit, as usual, to check up on how progress was going. The home entertainment contractor was pulling cable and hit the back of his hand on a frame bracket that would hang a large screen TV.

Roger's presence still being unbeknownst to him, he yelled out in pain "Effen bracket!" Of course, he did not use "Effen" but used the actual word that begins with that. Like I said, I'm trying to keep this G rated.

Roger came up behind him and yelled, "Hey, nobody uses the word bracket in my house!"

So, for the rest of this book, if you see bracket symbols, it is my way of using creative verbiage stemming from this moment in time.

Back to the past...Shortly after my first Holy Communion at age 7, we moved to Jamaica Plain. A little suburb off of Boston. There was a lovely little cemetery at the end of our street... a cemetery surrounded by a forest that I almost burned down...

Paul Joseph Brennan

Chapter 2

Jamaica Plain

I was in my eighth year on planet earth and Seventy-three Tower Street was a magical place to live! At that time, I found that the closer you got to the end of the street the tougher the kids got. Some of the toughest people I know are dead, so it made sense that Forest Hill Cemetery was located at the end of the street. The Averil's lived right against the cemetery's picket fence. They were great friends; one of the older brothers was the toughest jarhead in town, down to the younger ones, street kids. They introduced me to cigarettes by the time I was eight. And why not? I was already addicted to beer, courtesy of my Uncle.

The twin Leanard brothers, who also lived on that street, were always fighting, mostly each other. I was glad for that because otherwise they would be kicking my butt. Their older brother looked just like the sergeant on the weekly series "Combat" and that's exactly what we played every weekday after school. We met out in the center of the cemetery where two-thirds of the miles of property were forest. The cemetery had private security police to watch over it. One guy, named Daryl, was to be feared!

I think he was like an old, World War I vet that had taken the war-games home with him. It kind of made our game feel real! If we could have painted his cobalt blue station wagon with gray Nazi swastikas we would for sure have been dead instead of merely scared stiff! No, really! When he'd show up, you'd freeze! *Like Christopher Reeve did in the movie* Somewhere in Time *when he discovered a penny while back in time!*

That blue wagon ended wars, baseball games and tobogganing. Come to think of it, Daryl probably *let us* sled down "Bloody Hill" because of its name. Either he didn't want to chase us in the snow or he just wanted to count how many trees had blood stains by the time he would lock the gate for the night. It was all fun and games, until the night my older brother, Bobby, and I almost burned the cemetery down playing with our cap guns and dried pine needles.

We would gather the pine needles and light them on fire inside a bucket, then drop the caps in. If it made such a fun noise dropping in several caps, then dropping a few rolls in should be even better, right? This was our logic! So, that's what we did. The burning needles quickly erupted into an explosion that ignited the surrounding brush, overwhelming our ability to control the flames. The fire was spreading fast! Running all the way home to bring back a few glasses of water was futile! By the time we had returned, the fire had spread and several fire trucks were at the scene of the crime. Needless to say, this scared us into running back home to hide!

Unfortunately, my sister saw us running our glasses of water in the direction of the fire and figured things out. She used this as blackmail. Our payment to keep it a secret? Doing her turn of washing the dishes for weeks. It must have worked, because we never did get found out for the cemetery fire.

Daryl wasn't the only scary man in Jamaica Plain; we had a neighbor named Mr. Gabee that wasn't too fond of the neighborhood kids. He was always chasing us away from the front of his house. He wanted us to stay away, but that was impossible, as he was the second house from the end of a dead-end. Everyone who came up that street had to use that driveway between the Averil's house and his to turn around.

We would also play half ball right there and he would always chase us off. One day, he went too far and hit my brother Bobby. My dad was on crutches at the time, with both knees in a cast. The blade on the bulldozer had pinned him against a wall and broken his knees. But that didn't stop him from facing off against Mr. Gabee! When he found out that Mr. Gabee had hit Bobby, he went up on both crutches and headed down the street.

Up the porch stairs he went in a rage. When Mr. Gabee answered the door, both crutches flew! He pinned Gabee up against the wall over his head, while me and the neighborhood kids all chanted "Hit him, hit him!" or "Kill him, Mr. Brennan"! Dad slammed him against the wall several times with a warning to never touch his kid or any other kid on the street, ever again! Retrieving his crutches, the cheers started and didn't stop until Dad made it all the way home. Heroism isn't without its consequences though, by the time he walked through the front door, he said he was hurting pretty badly because the adrenaline rush was going away!

By the time I turned eleven years old, Brennan Trucking (my dad's company) had the opportunity to contract for the expansion of the Logan International Airport. This was a fantastic opportunity for my dad. Unfortunately, he also took on a crooked partner who took a lot of the money that our family never saw. There were many arguments in the Brennan home that most of the neighborhood could hear. All the kids playing stickball in the street would cheer as my dad would leave because of the way the tires on the car would smoke and screech halfway down the street! I remember Dad always had really nice cars; one in particular was a Bonneville convertible.

After one particular fight, I knew a storm was on the horizon. The thunder in my head was getting really loud... we're moving again...

Chapter 3

Stoughton...Trained in the Art of Forced Deception

Between my addiction to tobacco and alcohol and increased violence at home, my outlook on a lot of things changed and the innocence of my childhood vanished. I no longer referred to my dad as "Dad," instead he became "Geno" or the "old man." His fights with mom became so abusive and loud it definitely carried over in the way she treated us.

Dad's job, coupled with all the pressures at home, kept him away a lot. He would leave and come home every other weekend. Then, eventually his coming home every other weekend turned into every other month. Money was scarce and the phone seemed to ring too many times a day. We were taught to tell bill collectors that my parents were not home. All the while, one or both of them would be standing in front of us mouthing what to say. It was just plain terrifying to know that if I said something wrong the beatings would begin.

It was in these days that Mom got a job and Dad rarely showed up. It was up to us kids to be responsible for cleaning the dinner dishes and the dirty diapers. It was difficult but doable because Stoughton was just an awesome place to live. I was twelve and I had a crush on a beautiful Irish girl by the last name of Daughtry. She didn't know about my feelings for her, so it was a private crush.

Her older brother hung out with my brother and we all played hockey together, but I couldn't bring myself to invite her into that circle. It seemed awkward. She sure was pretty though. I would occasionally walk home with her and we would talk a little bit about schoolwork and teachers and some of the students. I just could never get up the courage to ask, "Can I carry your books?" or "Can I hold your hand?".

It was around this time in my childhood that I broke my collarbone playing touch football. The pain was excruciating; though not compared to the hurt when my kid brother backed up, jumped and landed, sitting down on my mending shoulder. He didn't do it on purpose, he was just trying to re-enact a Batman move on television and got carried away. That was a rough night babysitting! Compound fracture the second time, right through the skin. It had to be reset and immobilized, to the point where I needed help going to the bathroom. Now that was embarrassing!

A broken bone is a pretty hard thing to go through, but even more difficult was the fact that my mother had started asking if we wanted to live with her or my father. I was crushed! I felt like my heart was broken, as well! I was scared, and I didn't know how to answer, so one night I said "both." She turned and closed the door to my room and walked away. I don't think I slept that night. It was during that same week that something ominous happened! Something that could only be explained in an Alfred Hitchcock movie!

My mom, either through the loss of her spouse or their mutual hurt feelings, had become very inquisitive about spiritual things and God. This went on for a long time but what was crazy was the unexplained attack against me from an unseen enemy from a world that I knew nothing about at that age!

Some of my mother's new friends at work had invited her to a healing meeting and one specific friend had a birth defect. One of her legs was shorter by 3 inches than the other and she had to wear a corrective heal in her shoe so she could walk without a limp. At this faith meeting, she was completely healed and walked out holding her shoes in her hand and no limp. She walked normal! Now, whatever it was from these meetings that my mom was messing around with she brought home with her. It scared me to the point that I thought of death and I did not even understand death. I just knew I did not want to be in the room with whatever it was that was holding me bound, pressing me into the bed.

I had no ability to cry out for help or to free myself. Any attempt was futile. I had no ability to turn, not even my head to look away or to scream for help in the panic that I was in! After the space of what seemed forever, this enemy which held me bound let go and I heard the springs on my mattress squeak. I rose from my bed quickly and made it into the bathroom. I turned on the light and just stared into the mirror, not wanting to go back into my room. I was afraid of the return of this unknown force or, if I had just been dreaming, I did not want to go back to sleep and have that dream ever, ever again!

My mom sought out several other churches to find answers that she was not getting from Catholicism. As she would study and read, she would come up with more questions that could not be answered. Time and again, she was told "all will be made known in the end, just have faith". I found out much later in life that the night I was bound towards destruction, my mother was also attacked by that unseen enemy.

As teenagers, we would talk about Ouija boards and make fun of them, but respectfully after that night I wanted nothing to do with that crap. And it gave me chills when I would hear haunting stories that were possibly just made up, but nonetheless I had a baseline to go off of that I never wanted to go anywhere near again. We also used to go out in the yard at night and look at the stars in the heavens and talk about potential aliens. We truly gave those thoughts a lot of energy! Then, of course, the movie "War of the Worlds" started to affect my optimistic views of visitors, going more towards the negative.

There's not much on the positive side to say about this time in my life. It was basically survival and a hope that somehow things would get better in time. Kids shouldn't have that much responsibility forced on them; to have to live in such a grown-up world at that early age. I believe that kids should have chores and participate in family life, but my world at that time was so full of negative that it was rough. All we had to look forward to was Saturday morning cartoons. My desire to watch cartoons shows that I was still a little kid while having to take care of little kids. Being a little kid in a miserable situation, I didn't even realize that my mom must have been suffering the same or worse.

Her misery came out against us, because she had no one else to vent to. She would physically and mentally take out her stress and depression on us if the dishes weren't done, or the house was a disaster. No wonder she was looking for religion. It was either religion, or alcohol. Her mother was such a horrible drunk when mom was a child, she was vehemently opposed to becoming like her. I guess that was one negative cycle she was able to break.

Speaking of breaking things… my penchant for breaking bones at an early age gave me a unique sense of humor. Although, not that unique when it comes to being a protective father raising daughters. Most fathers threaten, with guns and knives, the boys who dare come around. The old "polishing and cleaning the weapon" bit.

My favorite was to give them a questionnaire and contract for them to sign. I know how a boy's ego works and what can inspire fear in a young boy's mind. One of my favorite questions on the dating questionnaire was "If you were to have one bone broken on your body, which would be your last choice?" Some would say the neck, but I know a compound fracture of the collar bone, twice within a week, would be my personal choice!

I used this contract with my son-in-law when he was dating my eldest daughter. He "one-upped" me though and changed the wording on the contract, which he signed, to say "marry my daughter" instead of "date my daughter". The bone he chose to want broken the least? *None!*

Another job, another move, for our dysfunctional family. This one, now 100 miles away in Springfield, Massachusetts, changed everything. If there was ever any pixie dust of make-believe left in my life, it now seemed far distant. Now the reality of desegregation was in my school and the racial riots and fights had started right in junior high school. What was absent when we went to private parochial school was now in my face every day.

In parochial school, when we would get off the overhead train and notice the police in riot gear, this meant we had to cross the street and get on the next train home. No school for us during the riots! I was actually hopeful to see those officers in riot gear because, at school, Sister Saint Rose would usually just lock me in the closet that went down to the basement, which was pretty "{ }" weird and scary! Not a good idea to put an angry nun with a kid who stood in need of medication just to be able to pay attention, but who knew back then? I was not an unruly child, I just didn't catch on. I also wasn't very social; I don't remember ever really talking to many of the kids sitting around me.

I do remember junior high and fighting two black guys that always hung out together and always took everybody's lunch money. When it came to my turn, I would never give them my money. I would rather fight and I did! When it came time to fight, I had absolutely no fear of what they could do to punish me. Every time they would demand my money, I would give them my fist as fast and as hard and as often as I could swing until somebody stopped us from swinging at each other. They should have been able to kick my butt because they were bigger than me and there were two of them. They would never fight me alone, only in pairs. Maybe what they couldn't figure out is how to hurt somebody who's conditioned to receiving a lot of beatings!

Because of the violence going on at the schools, the National Guard began showing up at our junior high school in Forest Park every day to get everybody out and on their way back home safely. I started to realize it was just easier to skip school than to deal with this every day. I would walk in late, sign in at the office and walk out the other door. I skipped about 180 days of school in seventh grade, my last year of formal education. It actually became a learned skill to avoid truant officers and hideout eight hours a day and get food and cigarettes. I got very creative!

My mom continued in her quest to find spiritual answers. The miracles and/or wonders of charismatic preachers and events were so powerful it actually inspired my mom to drive hours in the pouring rain, by herself, down the Massachusetts Turnpike from Springfield to Boston. She really felt inside that there was no explanation for those healings and manifestations, except that God had to be involved. As weird and as uncomfortable as she felt, she could not deny it. So, she said a prayer in desperation, wanting to do the right thing but fearing her entire belief system was being turned upside down.

The prayer she offered was simple and much different from the prayers of Catholicism's history at that time in 1972. She committed to God that she would go and join this specific Church who believed in baptism by immersion if He would make everything work out just right to help comfort her frayed emotions.

Upon arrival, her brother-in-law, who was supposed to meet her, was not there. For her, this was the first red flag with sirens blasting because things were not going smoothly. "What do you mean my brother-in-law is not here?" A former Catholic priest that had quit Catholicism and joined this church said that he would be happy to baptize her and then her brother-in-law would give her the gift of the Holy Ghost by the laying on of hands when he was back in town the following Wednesday night.

My mom's main criteria was baptism by immersion by someone holding God's authority to do that. In this specific church, the focus was on the gift of the Holy Ghost and speaking in tongues and rolling around on the floor consumed by the Spirit of God, as well as healings at the meetings from all diverse kinds of problems people have in this world of physical pain and suffering. So, the perfect counterpoint to her desire to be baptized in this church was the former Catholic priest saying, "Don't worry Mary, I'll baptize you now and your brother in law will finish the job on Wednesday!"

"No, you won't" she said as she stormed out of that chapel. She got in her car and drove the two hours back home in the pouring rain. Hydroplaning made that whole trip scary and unsafe.

I don't care who you are, if you blow-off Mary Brennan, you're going to hear about it! This time standing on the front porch in Springfield, she stomped her foot and raised her fist, shaking at the heavens above. Loud enough that all the neighbors could hear, she yelled, "I drove two hours to Boston, damn near lost control several times, my brother-in-law was not there, nothing worked out right today. I don't know what I am supposed to do! I don't have a phone, so you can't call me, they pulled it last week for lack of payment, so you're just going to have to ring my bell!" And with that, she stormed into the house, slamming the door behind her and slapping the Bible down onto the kitchen table in tears!

You've got to know that the landlord of the planet Earth, Heavenly Father, definitely has a sense of humor! It was the very next morning that I was rudely awakened by two Fed's standing there! I was scared to death. Guilt overwhelmed me. Even if there was no reason, I was used to feeling guilty for everything. Going through the motions of greeting them at the door, but not wanting to, I heard one of them say, "We need to talk to your mother, is she home?" As he said this, he flipped a white wallet at me then quickly closed it and put it back in his top pocket.

"What do you need her for," I asked.

The guy next to him punched him in the arm and said, "We're missionaries from the Church of Jesus Christ of latter-day Saints".

As soon as I heard "missionaries," the pressure that held me bound was lost. I was now free to go back to the couch. I said, "Religion?... she's in the kitchen, knock yourself out." I dove onto the couch before I finished that sentence. Now, knowing full well I was not caught, I was totally relieved and went right back to sleep.

After this first meeting, the missionaries kept coming by for months. One time, they even taught us how to make tacos. I thought, "Who gives a crap about tacos?" They sure did, and they were so happy to teach us about them. We had never heard of tacos before that.

My friends and I thought these dudes were gay because of

their appearance... always in suits and ties, and they were always together. They lived up the street and we had to bring them food all the time. My mother would feed them because they were away from home and away from their families so she felt bad for them. She didn't feel bad enough to join them, only to let them come visit or to feed them; that's where she drew the line.

She, like me, never wanted to have an experience like the one she had when she was going to all the TV evangelist meetings. That was too real and far too dark! Not the things that she saw in the meetings; those were so illuminating and bright and surreal. The rolling around on the floor was a little uncomfortable for a Catholic who mostly just politely kneels and stands and lights candles and messes with rosary beads and talks to men behind curtains. OK, it's starting to sound weird too, but the stuff that happens when you're all by yourself and you invite death if delivery does not show soon enough... that's the stuff nobody needs! "{ }" EVER! So, rather than be "tricked" again, she wouldn't allow a more personal meeting, such as dinner with the missionaries.

In Springfield, our house was between the two big gangs, the X gang, which I should've belonged to because they were Irish, and the other gang who were all Italians. My best friend moved south from my section of town, so we hung out with the Italians or the South End gang at Mo Mo's corner coffee shop.

At this time, there was a group of long hairs that lived next door on the top floor and my mom used to feed them. I didn't know it but they were all college graduates and owned a PA system. I ended up helping them with free concerts in the park on the weekends and it turned into a full-time job.

Shortly after I started working with them, they moved to an upper middle-class neighborhood, because of the success with their concerts. In fact, at one point in our career, we were doing Concerts East when Don Kirshner was doing Concerts West and the Friday night show on TV. We staged all the big bands in all the convention centers.

A class act was Dizzy Gillespie and the Ink Spots, as well as Arthur Fiedler and the Boston Pops. We had even more fun with Cheech and Chong Live, Savoy Brown and the James Gang, NRBQ and John Sebastian. Leslie West and Mountain... Dozens and dozens of local bands across Connecticut, Cape Cod, Holyoke, Amherst, the Springfield Convention Center, etc.

That's when I got my ear chopped off by one of the neighbors who did not like all those "long hairs" living next door...

Chapter 4

The Good, the Bad and the Ugly!

We had just gotten back from a softball game and I was unloading the U-Haul into the basement with all the 4 x 4 base speakers, cable boxes, stack horns and staging equipment that ran some very large bands.

It was during this that the neighbor kept calling his friend, the captain of the local police department to come and hassle us for existing. After the third visit, the officer was somewhat embarrassed when I asked him where he first heard the annoyance of our music and he had to answer honestly that he didn't hear it until he got to the front door.

The 45-year-old drunk across the street was back from the VFW club feeling bulletproof and one of my friends went over to ask, "Please contact me and I'll be very happy to shut my music off if it's bugging you, but it was not even loud enough to annoy the cops." While he was at their front door, the old man and his son jumped him and started to beat on him out in front of their house. I saw this and ran over to assist my friend. I took on the son who was a college boy.

I was a large 14-year-old with an attitude of jump in and ask questions later. The fact is, my job after building and stacking the PA system was to kick guys even bigger than him off the stage when they were drunk and tried to climb on to party at concerts… boom, boom, out go the lights! My mistake here was a war cry warning them of my charge. It was kind of comical as I ran right into his straight-arm fist. My feet went right out from under me, but as fast as I went down I got up and grabbed him from his side and bear hugged his arms useless. With his legs, he was smashing me against the telephone pole, but he was losing energy quickly. I was not only a cling-on, I was squeezing his ability to breathe and working his balance with my legs wrapped around his. All the while knowing my friend and boss (I'll call him Rob) would drop the old man and come take this menace off my hands.

All of that came to pass. Rob put the hurt on the dad and the dad ran to his garage to get a weapon. Rob pulled us apart and I ran to the back of the station wagon where the softball equipment was. How convenient... an aluminum bat! I returned to the street painted line and yelled out how I would use the bat to end it now. The son retreated and Rob commanded me to put the "{ }" bat away.

Assuming it was over, I walked towards Rob's house, when Desilveroni (the dad) ran up behind me swinging at my neck with a hatchet! I ducked but only quick enough to stop his swing with the side of my head. BAM! The next thing I saw was bright lights and lots of colors, while he was winding up for the next hit! Luckily, the hatchet missed my chest and was sticking into the ground behind me as I continued to roll. I was up and on my feet in no time, facing the front door of Rob's house, dragging the bat, bewildered as to what just happened.

Screams were coming from the girls who were pointing at me, one gagging. All the white roses on my black & white shirt were red, with blood. As I flipped my hair off my shoulder, a piece of my left ear fell off! Almost as fast as it hit the ground, Bandit, my friend's half husky Shepherd was chewing it. Carly, one of the girls who witnessed this scene, lost her lunch. Rob thumped Bandit's head and he dropped my ear back onto the floor. Before it hit the floor the second time, my senses returned and I knew what had just happened to me. I raised my bat with two hands and charged out the door to the enclosed porch.

I had one foot on the deck when Rob grabbed my belt from behind, pulling and jerking me air-born backwards until I crashed into the wall /door frame dividing the staircase entry way into the dining room. A second blow to my head! I was losing steam as I slid down the wall until I was in a squatting position and then I asked for a beer and a smoke. I was spent!

While the girls went got napkins to pick up my ear, Rob was on the phone calling the police. They were on the front lawn in no time, their headlights bouncing from jumping the sidewalk when they heard what had happened! I was rushed off to the hospital with my head gushing blood and adrenaline pumping; my blood pressure was way up. They wouldn't give me any medication for pain because they couldn't tell how many beers I had consumed! Let me tell you, it hurt like a "()'#$&%*'" when they were sewing my ear closed and gave me 9 stitches in my skull.

One of the girls must've called my mom, because here comes Mary prophesying, "Show me your friends and I'll tell you who you are!" Yeah, I'm a 14-year-old, working my job unloading the truck and the crazy drunk neighbor from World War II figures it's starting over again and he's going to kill us commie b@#$%*d's. All he wanted to do is bury the hatchet! *Pun intended!*

Interestingly, *he* took *us* to court... and lost. The judge interrupted Desilveroni's testimony with a question of who bit Brennan's ear off? Everybody laughed.... Except for me. At this point, I envisioned him handcuffed to a burning car... or at least 5 minutes alone with me so I could bring my own kind of justice!

My friend Rob went on to be very successful in the insurance industry, top in his career. My mom went back to school and became a nurse. Waitressing was just not cutting it. And it was during this time in my life that my dad was in prison. I remember one of my biker friends taking me out to Danbury State Penitentiary. I wanted to find out how much trouble I could be in if I was dumb enough to mess with that drunk Italian neighbor again. Even at age 14 I knew not to take chances. Not that I had to kiss my father's ring, but my dad was definitely well-connected. So much so, in fact, that the Feds claimed he was making too much money. I mean big money. So big, that…well, let's just say it was a quarter of an inch too big!

This earth life is so wonderfully mapped out, and yet we have agency to give us different scenery. Now the scenery that my dad chose from his extracurricular activity put him behind bars, but only for a short while if you think of the bars he'd be behind if he would've killed that drunk neighbor for chopping his 14-year-old boys' ear off! Well, whatever he was doing, the Feds have a way of doing it right back. My dad said they put counterfeit plates in his vehicle when they pulled him over, and instead of turning evidence and becoming a 🐭 SPIONE 🐭, he did the time…3 -5 years!

This was my dad's favorite joke; well, one of the few that I feel okay to repeat.

Question: What do you get when you take the "F" out of the word "justice"? Say the answer out loud to catch the meaning.

After my dad got out of prison, his favorite business was his Limo service with a 1959 Angel Cloud Rolls-Royce. Even though he ran from the idea of holy matrimony after my mom, having his pearlescent white, burgundy interior Rolls-Royce for the bride's car, he just fit the role! His business card said, "Above the rest" and he really was! He would meet every schedule. Everybody loved having him on that memorable day because he was a class act, no doubt about it. When the downtown Boston traffic hit, he would roll down his window, wave his umbrella and stab it at other cars who would come too close to that pearlescent paint job! I am sure there are brides in Boston that have video footage of this. That was just his personality and I miss him.

In the movie "Analyze This", Billy Crystal is making fun of Robert De Nero with "I'm sure you're not accustomed to hearing the word *no* from people," and De Niro came back with "Quite the contrary! I hear it a lot! In fact, it's followed by 'Please no! No please! Please no, noooo!'." That was like my dad. My dad even looked a lot like De Niro. His facial expressions were very similar! He was also a combination of Charlie Rich and the Man from Glad…especially because of the tux and the white hair.

He graduated from planet earth about eight years after my mom. But more about that in another chapter…

Back home at the ranch, Mom and her Kitchen Bible had many great debates with the young Mormon boys from Utah. In fact, a lot of these guys were scholars in the Old Testament, as well as the New Testament. When one missionary would move out of the area, new transfers would keep coming. One guy even had a degree in Latin. Detective (Elder) Weaver was the only guy that never got a transfer, which is odd because it's usually a see-saw and the older guy breaks in the new guy and then gets transferred to a new area.

After many months of visiting with Elder Weaver and each new companion he happened to bring with him, he came up with this inspired rejection…

Elder Weaver: "I'm sorry Mrs. Brennan but we can't come back to your house and visit anymore!"

Mom Brennan: "You guys have been coming for months,

why now? You just give me your mission president's phone number and I'll give him a piece of my mind!"

Elder Weaver: "It's not him. He has nothing to do with this, this is our decision to move on."

Mom Brennan: "You can't do this to me! You guys are the only thing that I look forward to! My kids could give a damn about religion and you guys are so full of information and happiness when you're around. I can't explain it, but you can't just leave. What did I do to offend you? What can I do to change your mind?"

Elder Weaver: "We have come out for only two short years to share what's very dear to us, but you won't let us talk about it here in your home. You will not allow us to tell you about the Book of Mormon. In fact, you said you wanted the oldest religion and none of this new stuff. You wanted to go back to Judaism! We have to move on. We'll come back and be friends after our mission, but it's really taking up a lot of our time coming here. It's fun and everything but we're not doing what we came out here to do. You will not let us."

Mom Brennan: "Well, what can I do to change that? What will make you guys want to keep coming back? How can we fix this?"

Elder Weaver: "Let us teach you about the Book of Mormon."

Mom Brennan: "Well, if that's all it takes then go ahead!"

Two weeks after the introduction of the book of Mormon, where it came from, and of course, getting an answer to prayer, mom was baptized by immersion as a member of the Church of Jesus Christ of latter-day Saints. Also known as the Mormons, or the Latter-Day Saints or LDS, or as my dad would put it, the ones with all the wives...not true, by the way).

Now she knew, like Paul Harvey News, the rest of the story! Really simple... After Christ's crucifixion, Constantine replaced all the original pastors, evangelists, teachers and priests and killed the apostles who ordained these men, and then put his own men in their place. He then stopped being a sun worshiper and became a Christian because of how fearless these Christians had faced death. He wanted that fearlessness in his army.

But what happens to an organization set up by Deity and cut off from the face of the earth by man? Answer: The Dark Ages... the great reformers came and with all of their influence and wisdom, they knew that something was missing and they looked forward to the restitution of all things spoken of by the mouth of the Prophets since the creation of time down to the Savior himself prophesying his own graduation plan. Pretty cool story!

Before Elder Weaver got transferred, I became a Mormon by being baptized and as soon as I did I took on a new personality! The gang liked it and they started to call me Preacher Paul. I didn't get high on drugs with them anymore and when they came over wanting to go beat up members of the X gang, I would just have to mosey on home. It didn't last very long, though. In fact, I had my falling away moment with a friend who was smoking and it just smelled overwhelmingly too good. Unfortunately, my falling away from the church went really far. It seemed as though I had to make up for lost time.

I left that section of town, moved away from home, got my hair cut off and bounced around a small town called Munson. After a while though, I got involved with a small family who was just trying to help a mixed-up teenager make better choices and I was given a small miracle, better known as a Letter from Heaven. *Not really a "small" miracle, as it filled four sides of legal paper.* This is known as a patriarchal blessing. They were given in the Old Testament times to acknowledge the birthright, and declare which of the 12 tribes of Israel a person hails from.

The reason I'm going into detail here is that parchment of paper given me by Patriarch Jesse Clyde Sumsion, in Hartford Connecticut in 1972, had information that has come up several times in my life that actually saved me. Suffice it to say the written word of God can and will deliver you out of or into lion dens! It will either work for you, or against you. It's definitely sharper than a two-edge sword or even a hatchet!

While I was living in Munson, who would figure my family would deteriorate any further than it already had? In fact, the last thing I remember doing together as a family, including my dad, was going to see *Fiddler on the Roof*, the movie all about tradition! *How I loved Tevye!* That is the last family event we were all alive and together. It seemed like the next day everything went to hell. I remember when my father wanted to come and get me out of that house in Munson. In no uncertain terms, a promised back breaking was something I could look forward to if he showed up. I countered that with, "Fine, the shotgun is loaded and leaning against the front door. Come on."

Meanwhile, do you remember how I used to hang out with the South-End gang around Mo-Mo's corner coffee shop? Well, that ended abruptly when I found out that one night some guys beat the crap out of this kid that was a loner, just because he didn't belong to a gang. Well this kid happened to be my big brother, Bobby.

Bobby was just a big mild-mannered kid that refused to be forced into joining any gang. He liked to fix electrical appliances and spent a lot of his spare time tinkering with things. This beating started a brain tumor that eventually ended my brother's life. Bobby was only 17. I swore an oath that if, or when, I crossed the path of the guys that did this to my brother, I would kill them! My buddies in the gang warned them when they showed up to leave before I came out. They left, and when I found out, that ended my relationship with the South-end guys. Putting the "killer's" safety above our friendship was unpardonable.

While Bobby was in the hospital dying, our uncle came to give him a healing blessing. When he entered, he offered his hand to Bobby so that he could get his approval to give him a blessing. My mother felt darkness and tried to stop him, but she failed. He made it over to my brother and asked, "May I give you a blessing son?" Bobby blinked once, which meant no. Our uncle didn't know the sign though, so he took it as a yes and he tried to give him a blessing. He didn't notice Bobby's bedside guardian angel, my mother, in the doorway praying for him not to be able to give Bobby the blessing.

The blessing never happened because our uncle suddenly couldn't speak. Something else happened while this was going on. My mother witnessed my uncle's countenance change, as he struggled to speak and failed. She watched what happened to that beloved man that can only be explained in Ephesians.

"For we wrestle not against flesh and blood, but against principalities, against powers, against the rulers of the darkness of this world, against spiritual wickedness in high places" (Ephesians 6:12).

My uncle always had the biggest heart. He had always been our personal family hero! He quickly left the room when his voice returned, apologizing as he walked out. This had never happened to him before. He was frustrated and muttering to himself, because he had driven two hours to get to the hospital.

Later, while Bobby lay in the hospital bed, the LDS missionaries came to visit him. They talked about the Book of Mormon and Ancient American history and Bobby knew full well that the book of Mormon was a true record of pre-

Columbian civilizations that covered this continent. But he also had a deep-rooted desire for his dad to love him, and not make fun of him as he saw his mother being ridiculed. Before he lost his ability to speak, he shared this hurt inside with a friend named Cheryl. He told her, "I know that the Mormon religion has been restored to the earth, but I don't know how to deal with my father. So, my plan is to wait until I'm 18 years old next year and approach him with my decision to join and respectfully let him know that I don't need his sanction because I'm a man now, but I would love to have his blessing and his respect. Mom's not crazy!"

Sadly, Bobby passed away shortly after that. At the funeral, we had a lot of screwed up high school kids who didn't have any idea about the afterlife, and they were pretty torn up over Bobby's passing. Then there was the "Mafia" meeting in the back because that's the only place for parolees to get together. But then you had these wonderful selfless Latter-Day Saints (Mormons) that were in a take-charge kind of mode. They had organized a luncheon for everyone who traveled out of town to be there. They took care of the flowers and the eulogy. They were a wonderful support team and they mixed well with the owners of the funeral home.

Cheryl sat next to my mother in tears and fought her way through her emotions to let my mother know of my brother's ambitions and that sadly they would never be fulfilled! My mother comforted her the best she could and thanked her. The graveside service ended and everybody went home. Dad to his place in Boston, mom to her place in Springfield, and Bobby to his new place awaiting the return of all of us.

But Bobby's story was not quite over! You see, one year after the graveside prayer and grave dedication, above 12 Stone Oxen facing in four separate directions, a baptismal font filled with water and a staircase leading down into that font, a young man entered and was immersed in that water.

Acting by proxy in Bobby's name, he was baptized by immersion by one holding the authority of God in God's temple on this earth. Bobby finally became a member of the Church of Jesus Christ of Latter-Day Saints!

Paul Joseph Brennan

Chapter 5

Utah…Really? Utah?

With her husband gone and her anchor, my oldest brother Bobby, gone, and seeing her family slowly falling apart, Mom Brennan was inspired to move to Utah. With two drugged cats, two brawling energetic young boys, and a teenage daughter, all stuffed into a nineteen sixty something wood panel rust framed Ford Station Wagon, they headed for the hills… of Utah.

I had received a phone call the day before that alerted me to the fact that what was left of my family was leaving for Utah with or without me, depending on if I showed up wanting to go. I decided that I needed to go with them to make sure they got to Utah safe. I wouldn't be able to forgive myself if something happened and I wasn't there to help; Over 2000 miles in an old well-used car.

When I showed up, I was surprised to see that everything from the house was sold. Everything in the car was symmetrically fitted and they were ready to roll at 8:00 am. I got there and jumped in, just as they were driving away. The drive was long and boring! Hours and hours, including several hotel stays, drugged cats and all. Four nights later, we rolled in to Lehi, Utah. All of a sudden, we felt a jolt where the tongue weight of the two-year supply of wheat my mom had brought finally had its toll on the rusted frame. We had to spend the night on the off-ramp to Lehi.

When the sun broke into the sky the next morning, I got out of the car and experienced something I can only describe as eminent death! The entire horizon in front of me was cut in half by a mountain of unfathomable depths of ocean! Ok, we all know that Utah doesn't have an ocean, but this city boy has never seen a mountain. Those Utah mountains fill the whole sky and driving in at night everything was dark so I didn't see it. Suddenly in the light of day, it took my breath away long enough to scar my memory forever!

When we arrived in Utah County, we moved in with some friends that had a large Mormon family who'd previously moved from Springfield to Utah. The meals were the most interesting to see in our new home, in military fashion. The bread was laid out for sandwich meat to then be collated with cheese and condiments. This went on for two weeks. Then my mom found a mobile home. Getting settled in was not on my plate of desire. I had no plans to stay in this State. I had a chip on my shoulder and it didn't matter how nice the people were, I wanted to get back to my life back east. The obligation I had felt was over with and I became very self-centered. It was time for me to go.

I told my family I was leaving and I could tell it was breaking my mother's heart. To just disappear without saying anything would have been easier, but it didn't work out that way. I had to tell her. I packed my bag and started out the door, as she said, "Wait a minute, what are you going to do for food and money?" I told her it didn't matter, I just needed to leave. She loaded me up with a loaf of bread, a jar of peanut butter, and $40, so I wouldn't get busted for vagrancy.

The mobile home we'd moved into was several blocks from Interstate 15, however, my mother insisted on taking me the long way to the mouth of Provo Canyon to see me on my way. I'm sure it was to spend as much time with me as possible. The voices in my head were screaming to just get out of the car. As much as I loved my mother, the chip on my shoulder was the size of Texas, and I felt there was nothing she could have done to keep me there!

As I was walking backward with my thumb out to hitch a ride, my thoughts were screaming to the passing drivers, begging them to please pick me up. Get me out of here! My mother was watching from her car. Suddenly she ran over to me with a small piece of string, thinking it might help to tie some of my things together. She just wanted to hug her 15-year-old son one last time. She had no idea when or if she'd see me again. I loved my mother, and I told her that! I didn't really know why, but I had to get out of there!

Finally, after what seemed an eternity, a trucker stopped to pick me up. She was still watching in her rear-view mirror.

The guy that picked me up was a guy that needed a lumper to help him unload furniture. He paid me to help. He was an owner-operator. I was with him only for a few weeks when the tie rod broke, and he lost control of the truck. We hit a culvert and I went through the windshield. I had some bad bruises, but otherwise okay. I was given severance pay and I put my thumb out again for the next phase of my journey.

Texas highways have a lot of rattlesnakes! It took me 3 days to get through Texas with rides here and there. Within weeks of returning to New England, I found myself at the Harbor House Hotel in Revere, Massachusetts, where I worked as a valet and a bar-back at night. During the day, I worked as an upholsterer in a Greek upholstery shop and learned the old-school way of putting a web spring back into chairs, love seats and couches. I worked so many hours everywhere that I barely got any sleep, but that changed when I went from the parking lot to the service bar & became a bartender. I covered on breaks, until I got my own schedule, then everything changed again when we went to open the Commodore Ballroom in Lowell, Massachusetts.

This place was for the big band era, what you'd find on "American Idol" or "The Voice"; a place for music artists to show off their talents. It was at this time that I met a waitress at the club that I wanted to get to know better and hopefully have a relationship with. In those days, in the night-club environment, it seemed the thing to do for a date was Chinese food. Most likely because they were always open after midnight when we were finished working. So, I asked her if she was hungry and she said, "Sure".

We went to her place for her to change because all the waitresses in those high dollar clubs wore fancy evening gowns. As she came out of her room dressed in more casual clothes, she said she wanted to "read my cards" before she went to dinner with me. I jokingly replied, "I'm an Aries". I figured that would tell her enough about me to move on to get food, but she refused and let me know that this was not just a passing fad for her. This was her way of life. She made all of her decisions based off of this belief system.

When she went through her specific process, she turned seemingly cold and told me she wouldn't date me because I would be leaving town in two weeks. When I assured her she was wrong, and that I was not going anywhere as I had a good position in the company and was happy where I was, she said, "I can tell you don't believe me. Not only are you leaving in two weeks, but you will reside in the Rocky Mountains and you will go on a sacred mission for God." I decided that she was crazy, but I wanted to prove to her how wrong she was. So, I asked her if she would go out with me if I was still here after two weeks. She agreed.

To my surprise and dismay, not long after that, things changed quickly. The car entrusted to me by the owner of the club became un-returnable when it ended up stuck to a telephone pole with the headlights looking at each other. The top of the pole broke off, and my friend who was driving begged me not to admit to anything. The blood that was pouring down my forehead helped me to play out amnesia. But after a week, the CEO was being harassed by the local authorities who wanted the club shut down and were going to use me to do it, as they knew I was underage and I was working there as a bartender.

So, the next time I showed up to work, guess what I was given? Severance pay and an airplane ticket for Kentucky, where my dad was working and living at the time. No worries…. Just one more move in the life of Paul.

Answer to the joke on page 37… There is no "F in justice". You've got to say it out loud.

My sentiments exactly!

In Kentucky, not quite eighteen yet, I was promised a job on the computer line, where all the payouts are made on horse betting at the derby. So, I bought a car and decided to drive back to Utah for a Christmas visit with mom and my sister and brothers. I hadn't seen or communicated with them for three years, but when I walked in at five in the morning, it was as if I had just left and came back in to grab my car keys. My mom somehow knew I was coming, only she was expecting me the next week, not that day. She really knew how to blow an entrance! No ticker tape. No confetti or surprise. But her love was ever present.

I had not written her a letter, nor had I answered any of hers, in those 3 years since I had left her at the mouth of Provo Canyon and hitched a ride back to New England. I had just thrown them all out one by one as soon as they arrived. Her handwriting was hard to read and I knew they would most likely make me feel guilty, so it was easier to not even open them at all. I had not even talked to her on the phone, nor had I told anyone that I was on my way to Utah. Yet she knew I was coming! Just like she had done 172 times before, catching me skipping school. She'd find me and say, "I see you're not going to school again! I'll see you when I get home."

I am not kidding. That lady found me every day I skipped school. I would be at a different place in the city and she would walk past me and wave and continue on to her college classes. I remember thinking it was not fair. It was like she had a built-in GPS to harass her son Paul. I know that our Heavenly Father has a sense of humor, because it was beyond crazy! Once or twice may be a coincidence, but this was multiple times a week, for months.

Back to the present, I was planning on staying in Utah for less than a month to visit during the holidays, but while I was getting ready to head back to Kentucky to fulfill my new career in computer training, I got busted by a local cop who pulled me over and pulled my car apart on University Avenue in Provo, Utah. Right in front of a music store, I got busted for possession, not of the devil, but of California and Colorado's now medically accepted pot. In my mind, it was no big deal at all, but in Provo, Utah, back in 1976, you would've thought I was Lee Harvey Oswald.

My mother came to bail me out. She was so delighted to have me home, she was walking on eggshells hoping I would stay; though she couldn't resist saying, "Show me your friends and I will tell you who you are." I had my harmonica and played "Tie a Yellow Ribbon." She went in and talked to the arresting officer, who went and got the sergeant. "You've got to hear this Sarge!" He and my parole officer listened to her plea... "If we can do anything to keep him and not make it so he'll become a fugitive"... She was begging for their help in being nice to me, knowing full well I would blow them off to never appear in Utah again.

They approached me with two options. Option number one, I would have to pay a fine and serve time in jail and it would go on my record; Option number two, go before the local high school board and let them decide my punishment and I would have to follow through with it. Which would it be?

I was told it would most likely be some type of restitution, which would not include a fine, jail time, nor would it go on my permanent record. I told them that I would gratefully take the freebie! I would have to appear before those high school kids where they would ask me any of the questions that came to their minds and I would have to answer honestly or do the time.

A date was set and I went before the board and behind me was the arresting officer, the sergeant, the detective, and my parole officer, who was very hot by the way! I was very faithful to my parole visits. She had a beautiful head of black hair that went way down past her waist.

The session was called to order by the sergeant, and the student body president was the first to ask questions about why I decided to do drugs. I answered that with, "In my neighborhood everybody did drugs. In fact, it seems like back east they treat drugs like a traffic ticket." Again, the student body president asked if I owned a car, wouldn't I want to put the drug money I spent into making my car better instead? "No."

A very attractive girl asked the next question. "Do you have a girlfriend?" I giggled a little bit and turned that into a potential date. She got a little embarrassed and before I made a mockery of this very cool situation I asked them if I could stop them for a moment and explain myself and they invited me to do so.

"You guys don't know lucky you are to live out here where everything still seems pure and good! I mean, back where I come from... the best way to put it is, if I could ask you a question..." I pointed at the student body President. "What would you do if your dad offered to blow a joint with you? Would you do it? I did with my dad and it was no big deal! Or how about you?" Pointing to someone else. "If the Sergeant here asked you to smoke a joint with him as he drove around looking for hippies to bust, would you do it? My best friend was a policeman and we used to drive around together and get stoned."

"And you," I pointed at another student. "I'm sure this would never happen, but if the Mayor of Provo offered, would you smoke with him? Well, I have smoked with mayors before when we had concerts and they had backstage passes in a lot of cities. So, what you have is something so pure. All I can say is that I want to give up all my vices. I really do! I want to stop all the drinking and the drugs, and I want to go on a mission for the church."

They were all very happy. They were smiling. Every one of them were taken by that moment and they let me know that they would get back with me on what the punishment would be for me to pay for my sins.

The meeting was adjourned, and my mother grabbed my elbow with her arm. Hugging me, she walked out of that courtroom in Provo, with the most loving, esteemed joyfulness. She was beaming! She looked into my eyes and said, "I am so proud of you!"

"Why?" I asked. "For pulling off that SNOW job back there?"

I watched as the confusion on her face melted into exasperated humor, before she said, "You b#$%&*d! You're just like your father!"

She could not control herself as she broke down into giggles that shortly became a full-blown belly laugh! We both laughed so hard that I was just hoping everybody was still doing high fives in the courtroom! I know it sounds heartless, but you need to understand the way I was brought up. One of my dad's favorite sayings was, "Don't let your right hand know what your left hand is doing!" Survival and self-preservation was instilled in us from the beginning. Heaven knew we needed it!

They let me know a few days later that they wanted me to watch a rehabilitation video about how a California teenager under the influence was rolling around in the sand under the boardwalk with an occasional wave of water washing against his legs! It was supposed to scare me away from doing drugs. Little did they know that I had seen much worse than that with my friends in my own life.

The very next day, a Mormon bishop by the name of **Leon Stubbs** stopped by my mom's mobile home with his counselor and gave my younger brother a blessing. They were finally able to meet this young man named Paul whom they heard so much about over the years from his mother. In that visit, Bishop Stubbs was trying to give good counsel and become a friend of mine.

He started to talk to me about my family and, in the few minutes of conversation, he touched on several things that pricked my heart. He'd never met my friend, the one who had given me the Patriarchal blessing those years before, which I secretly adopted as my dad because I wanted a dad like him. I wanted to be able to look up to a man that kept his covenants with his wife. A man that, when he spoke, you could feel not only his integrity and warmth, but you knew you were in the presence of someone who has daily two-way communications with Deity. Even though he'd never met him, the words he spoke to me that day were all too familiar and I knew I had heard them before.

Even though I had my sights set on money and my cool promised job, some ancient Irish blessing from my ancestors made for a compassionate sadness for the life that was dealt to my mother having to raise all of us with no help. As my emotions encircled this feeling, I made a choice to talk to God. I was looking up where the ceiling attaches to the wall, and my conversation went a little something like this…

"Dear God, I've made a decision to leave my family again, so unless you have some other plan for me, I'll be gone in the morning before my kid brothers wake up. If there's something that you want me to do, or if there's a reason you want me to stay here in Utah with my mother and brothers, you have to provide me with some kind of anchor that would hold the Titanic back from the iceberg, like the one that I know I'm heading for. You know my weaknesses and you know how I can make up for lost time. I know if I stay here, I'll not smoke or drink or anything else and that'll last for maybe three months or maybe even seven months, I don't know, but I do know it will end. And when that happens, all hell's going to break loose and I don't want to hurt my mother or my brothers like that ever again, so what will it be?"

I want you readers to know the truth. In my mind, I heard the voice of Patriarch Jesse Clyde Sumsion in his doorway, upon departing from receiving that very cool, very spiritual blessing those years ago, when I was only fourteen. "Paul, here is the copy of your blessing but I feel as though you're going to lose it, and I want you to know that a copy will be sent to the church office building in Salt Lake City."

He then proceeded to explain to me how to get a copy. My response at the time was, "Oh, I'll never lose this! That was such a spiritual enlightenment. I could never lose it. Thank you! Thank you so much! I love you." He then ruffled my hair with his fingers, knowing exactly what was going to happen. How sweet, how so exquisite this man's heart beat with the power of God. Through his veins flowed the wisdom of the great Creator!

Even though I did lose that copy of the recorded prayer, like he knew I would, with the information he had given me I was able to get a copy of it early the next morning. Then I drove an hour back home, with great anticipation for that afternoon, kneeling in prayer, begging for this to be my anchor. Filled with the sacred memory of its first pronouncement, the déjà vu effect became overwhelming to me. I unfolded this sacred blessing and, with the desire that I had for it to be my anchor, I read word for word what Bishop Stubbs counseled me just the day before, which had been written down in exactness, several years earlier by another servant of God, my friend, the Patriarch.

Even with the possibility of years of listening to a single-parent mother talk about her son and her daughter and her two other boys living with her, this Bishop could not have come up with the exact words that were written years earlier. Maybe some similar words could have been said that would be general counsel to a wayward youth. But separated by over 2000 miles and a few years, it was the miracle that I needed to change my life!

The feeling that I had in the center of my being radiated through every fiber of my cellular structure. I was overcome with such love, such peace. And just as this life changing patriarchal blessing promised me "…your heart will be filled with gladness and your pillow will be wet with tears of joy!", my eyes *were* filled to overflowing and my pillow became saturated with my tears!

That anchor has vibrated in this body 40 years now and counting! In fact, it has been challenged many times and I have come out to be the victor, by the tender mercies of God!

I have a book I treasure, titled "Leaves of Gold." It's like a Readers Digest of the greatest minds this world has ever known for poetry, positive thought and sublime contemplation on eternities' roll for every soul on this planet. Within the pages of that book lies my favorite quote.

"Only Once- We live but once. The years of childhood, when once past, are past forever. It matters not how ardently we may wish to live them over; it avails us nothing. So, it is with the other stages of life. The past is no longer ours. It has gone beyond our reach. What we have made it, it shall remain. There is no power in Heaven or on earth that can change it. The record of our past stands forth in bold and ineffaceable characters, open to the all-seeing eye of God. There it stands, and one day we shall give an account of it. The present moment alone is ours. Now is thy treasure possessed unawares. Today is a day which we never had before, which we shall never have again. It rose from the great ocean of eternity, and again sinks into its unfathomable depths."

— James E. Talmage

Chapter 6

A Yankee in Texas? Dallas

A friend of mine once, in his flatbed pick up with Texas plates, was delivering watermelons to a grocery store in Oklahoma. The front porch had a rocking chair filled with an anxious "pile of dust"; in other words, a very anxious, very old man who was giving my friend a deadeye stare. He was rocking back and forth, puffing on a pipe now and again. The pickup was two thirds empty before my friend broke the silence.

"Are you just going to sit there, or are you going to help me unload these watermelons?"

Looking at the Texas plates on the back of the truck and, assuming that all Texans must have had their finger on the trigger, that Okie took the pipe out of his mouth, squinted his eyes and said, "You the one that killed our president, incha?!"

My Texas buddy said, "Yeah and I'm fixing to get this one too!"

They both had a good laugh and got that truck emptied of watermelons. And that old boy emptied a prejudice that day, as well!

Well, as luck would have it, I was called to serve as a missionary for my church in the Texas, Dallas Mission April 1977 to April 1979. I love the people of Texas! And even though I'm a "Damn Yankee", a Patriots, Red Sox, Celtics, and Bruins fan, I love the people of Texas and I know they love me. At least the ones I met!

At times, it was a challenge when the meeting started out with "The damn Yankees burned down all the libraries and court houses so that their genealogy had come to a standstill" – then it was my turn to take the stand and testify of the truth and apologize for my ancestors! When you testify of the Lord Jesus Christ, you bury, or hide, a multitude of sins! So, Texas did me a lot of good. I'd had 20 years on planet earth and I left out all the times that I was held at gunpoint by different gangs or how I had driven through Springfield in stolen cars with loaded guns pointed at me by the X gang, mandating that I take out corner mailboxes; jumping curbs while the guns were loaded and jammed into my ribs and pointed in my face, yet I never got shot. Two years on a mission is time well spent. It's like tithing, ten percent.

My mission president, President Hart, was a retired admiral in the Navy. When he found out that I was from Boston, he took me aside to talk with him for probably an hour. Most missionaries got 10 minutes of his time, but he was just so happy that someone was not from Idaho, California or Utah, so he told me cloak and dagger stories from his life.

He told a story about how it was his job to oversee the building of the Polaris sub, America's first nuclear powered submarine in the Boston shipyard and the hassle he had with the union welders. He also told me how much he appreciated one particular sailor, a petty officer first class who was a paralegal. He gave him all the information required to get those union hands back to work every single time.

He also told me a story that will play a significant role later in my life. I will tell that story later, when it meant the most to me.

During my sojourn in Texas, it came time for my day in court to get justice for getting my ear cut off. I was on my mission now and I thought for sure that I would be told to turn the other cheek, let them cut the other ear off, so to speak... I'm a Bible thumper now! But my attorney called and requested I get permission to come back and go to court.

I knew that the leaders of my faith would frown on that, so I tried to break it to the attorney. He demanded that he needed me to follow through with this to recover some of the time and money that he had spent six years earlier on professional witness's, plastic surgeon's testimonies, etc. I promised him I would do what the prophet in Salt Lake City would tell me to do.

President Hart made the call to church headquarters. President Kimball, the prophet and president of The Church of Jesus Christ of Latter-Day Saints at the time, inquired if Desilveroni was a member of our faith. If he was, we could have a church court and handle it in-house. Of course, he was not a member.

President Kimball said, "Well, he won't listen to what we have to say, so take him to the courts of the land. Have Elder Brennan put his name badge away and represent himself in hopes that this Desilveroni repents of trying to kill Elder Brennan. No one should enter the next life with that emotion stuck in his or her soul. Maybe he could come clean of it in court."

We would hope. I had at an early age learned what courts were for...Courts of love and concern to help a person repent and become a better person, such as happens in our church; courts to play tennis or basketball... And civil and federal courts to also bring justice and give motivation for change... to repent and improve. I'm sure there are only a percentage of people that use this as motivation to become better, but in a perfect world, it would be great if all took advantage of this. Sadly enough, it seems that whoever has the most money to buy the better attorney, wins. Because of this, justice is not usually served, and people become hurt and angry and bitter.

This is where I could have very well become one of those bitter, angry losers! When in doubt, throw it out... and that's what they had to do because Desilveroni had 6 years to buy those expensive attorney's that would create doubt in the minds of the jury. Justice was not served that day, but the judge said something of prophetic utterance.

"There will be a time in the future when you the jury will be called back. A judge will be sitting here, and it will not be me, but a screen will show the actual event from that night and it will be viewed by all and that judge will pass the judgment and that's when justice will prevail!"

Gavel down, it was over. He won! But not really. He had his chance to get it off his chest and apologize and repent, or in other words, come clean with trying to kill a fourteen-year-old boy. You don't want to take that negative energy into the next life. I doubt it will go well for him.

I found myself thinking back to the time I wanted to handcuff this man to a burning car, or just to have five minutes alone with him to get my own justice. I went to the scriptures to find peace, as I had been accustomed to doing over the past year as a missionary. I had been teaching people how the young 14-year-old Joseph Smith had turned to the scriptures for an answer to his question and knew that I could do the same.

I turned to Romans 12:20 and I felt that it had much the same impact on me that James 1:5 had on Joseph when he read it. In fact, the emotion of anger and vengeance left me as I read this scripture. The apostle Paul was teaching me: "Therefore, if thine enemy hunger, feed him; if he thirst, give him drink: for in so doing thou shalt heap coals of fire on his head" (Romans 12:20). It was the apostle Paul that helped me put the fire in my heart out.

I learned so much on my two-year mission. It was a great time for a 24/7 education on God, myself and humanity. Up to this point, I had such a big chip on my shoulder from the way I had perceived life. To put it in technical terms, let's say I had PTSD. I had no idea that PTSD even existed, let alone had a name.

I was shell shocked by the feeling most of my life that someone was going to attack me at any moment. I was distrustful of people, constantly judging everyone to be on the take. I was always looking over my shoulder with very quick reflexes and always on guard. My two years in the mission field with fourteen different companions and fourteen different personalities, taught me more about humankind and kindness than any shrink could possibly have accomplished.

The Lord blessed me with the right combination of mission companions and their personalities and their issues, as well as their positive influences, to make me a better person. He knew exactly what I needed and when I couldn't handle anymore.

Once, I was watching and listening to a missionary give a talk at a zone conference. I was so embarrassed by his appearance and demeanor that I said to myself, "I would never want to have to hang around with him to introduce our church to anyone." I come from the polished background of New England's proper, as well as the night club facade where appearance is everything and this guy was just a dork in a nylon suit. I kid you not… by the next week, he was my companion! *Now all my companions are going to wonder if they were the one…but they'll always have to wonder because I'll never admit it!* It was a privilege to serve with this man and it was made known to me what an honor it truly was to serve with him. Who am I to judge people? My mission blessed me in more ways than I can count!

We did a little role-playing in the mission field with some

elders that were not really up to living all the rules. We broke into their apartment early in the morning, waking them up because they were sleeping in. We wore our suits and had masks on our faces and used a starting pistol with blanks. This worked quite well to wake each of them up from a dead sleep, thinking their companions were getting "iced"!

Although my mission was the best, all good things must come to an end. It was time to go home again; back to Utah after my mission.

Chapter 7

The Greatest Salesman in the World

There's no paycheck involved when you are on your mission. You must pay for it yourself, or get a family member to help pay for it and that's what my mom did. She worked as a nurse for her first full-time job and then managed a steakhouse some evenings during the week. The only time she slept was when you were trying to have a conversation with her!

She hired both my kid brothers to clean dishes in the kitchen at the restaurant. My sister worked as a waitress now and again. There was a girl named Karen that worked as the evening hostess and my mom kept telling her, "You're going to marry my son when he gets off his mission, so you can date until then but don't get serious with anyone!" Mom would also tell that to the guys that came in to flirt with this girl and she would just tell them that her boss was a crazy lady from Boston.

The parting counsel from most mission presidents to those going home is to get married and start a family sooner rather than later. When I got home from my mission, I went to the restaurant to visit my family one evening, as I was bored being home alone without my mission companion. Not that I'm needy or weird, but I was kind of lost at first. Two years of continually being around someone else 24/7 and now suddenly I find myself home and alone. As I walked in to the restaurant, Karen and I gained eye contact for the first time.

When she realized who I was, her first comment was, "Should we go on a date or just get married because your mom says?"

I had dated several other girls in the area and didn't know for sure who would marry me and put up with me. But as Karen and I started dating, we both seemed to know that we belonged together. Then I found out how old she was, or should I say how young she was! I didn't know how to overcome the age barrier because she was five years younger than me. I got off my mission when I was 21, so if you do the math you realize that I not only had to get her parent's permission, I almost had a fight with her bishop.

When I first learned of Karen's age, my heart sank and I knew that it more than likely was not going to work out for us. But there is something more than just man's wisdom taking place when your mother teases your possible future wife about how her son was going to marry her when he gets off his mission! Because of the persistence of my mom, I put more energy into trying to figure it out and I'm glad I did. By the time we dated for a few months, we became very close and I wanted to know for sure if she was the one that I should marry.

Under fasting and prayer, Karen and I went to the Provo Temple grounds to share our patriarchal blessings with each other. If you can imagine, it's the perfect background check. I don't think they had eHarmony websites set up for dating at that point in the year 1980. We sat on the grass together for a while and then said another heartfelt prayer. Words cannot express the flood of emotions that came over me when I opened hers and read what was at the top. The feeling I had must have been similar to how the boy prophet Joseph Smith felt when he read James 1:5, while searching for which church to join! Patriarch Jesse Clyde Sumsion's name was there! He had given Karen her patriarchal blessing.

He was my adopted spiritual dad. He'd lived over 2000 miles away, yet he had moved to Utah into the neighborhood near Karen's Family while I was on my mission. Karen had known this since our first date. We had sat on a rock and I had told her my story and told her about Jesse Clyde Sumsion and yet she hadn't told me! She was feeling pretty surprised at this information and, needless to say, it scared her a little! Okay… a lot! This was a first date with a guy that she had been told for a year that she was going to marry, by the guy's mother…

This is her story: When Karen and her brother set up appointments a few weeks before we met, to get their patriarchal blessings, her brother, Jon, had his appointment with a different patriarch. Karen had no idea who this Patriarch Sumsion was, so she called to change her appointment and get the same patriarch her brother had. While the phone was ringing she had a feeling to hang up and let it go.

She hung up and made the statement, "I'm sure they're all men of God and it doesn't matter who I have give me my blessing." This is how the Lord works. This is how he makes his will known to individuals who will listen and how nothing is left up to chance. When a sparrow falls to the ground, the heavens know it. The hairs on our head are numbered! *Mine are getting easier to count as the days go by.* At the time she hung up the phone, she had no idea that this would end up being an answer to my prayer of who to marry. She had no idea that this "Patriarch Sumsion guy" would end up being such a big part of her life in the future. But thankfully, she listened to the Spirit that told her to hang up the phone and not worry about it. This was an important event for our future. This was no coincidence!

The spirit was so strong that day at the temple that we

both knew without a doubt that we were meant to spend eternity together and fight whatever battles we needed to fight to get there. After that witness, there was nothing and no one that could change the outcome. The final answer was that she said yes and so did her parents. And finally, so did her bishop! He had a hard time with her age. I guess it was a big responsibility for him. He tried to pull the card that all this must be a sign from Heaven because he didn't sign her recommend in the right place. Kind of like saying, "You two should not get married right now."

So, I demanded of him, "Bishop if you were standing in front of me saying, 'Thus saith the Lord God Almighty', then so be it. But if you're just the guy down the street giving me your personal opinion, then sign the recommend and let us get on with our lives."

He re-signed the recommend correctly. I absolutely respect the office of Bishop, but we knew in our hearts that this was meant to be so I knew I had to question him on it. We were married a few months later in the Provo, Utah, Temple.

Working two jobs to bring in the money with not enough sleep was hard to do, so I certified with MSHA (Mining Health and Safety Administration) and prepared to go work for the real underground 8 miles under, Emery Mining Company in Emery County, Utah. No more working in the sweatshop making gun parts for Tallies North American Gun Manufacturing and then unloading trucks until 10, 11, 12 o'clock at night.

Karen had never lived away from her family. It was a big thing for us to pick up and move to another town, especially one three hours away from her home, but we were excited to start our own lives and become a family ourselves. In some ways, it was the best thing we could have done at the start of our marriage. It was difficult at times, and it was a very small town, but life was good!

Chapter 8

Eight Miles Underground

A little more risk involved in this job, but I got good sleep and made more money in eight hours than I did with the other two jobs I'd left. Now I had job security with health benefits and we could start a family in the small town of Castle Dale, Utah. A very small town in the middle of nowhere… well in the middle of the desert.

We were encircled by mountains and every day it took me 30 minutes to drive from the top of the mountain to work. Then we would travel 8 miles underground to where we were pulling pillars, making the earth cave behind us as we pulled out cross-sections of coal. It was high stress listening to the mountain settle and bounce! I worked in the coal mines for two and a half years and there, in Castle Dale, our first daughter was born. Tiffany Marie, our coal miners' daughter!

Construction people are generally average, blue-collar, "rough around all the edges," macho men (or women), ego driven, high stress, crude, rude and very stressed out kind of people. I'm not saying everyone… I'm saying generally. The management and bosses could be real ninny mongers. That's my favorite word to use to explain someone that's not really a nice person. *It reminds me of the word Will Ferrell uses in the movie* Elf, *only I think he called them "cotton headed ninny-muggins."* You see, my newfound language was more colorful than prison talk, but when you go underground you meet some of most interesting forms of life there! You have construction workers, but now they're encased and enshrouded in darkness for eight hours a day.

Coal mining is a high stress job, and dangerous! Underground, if you had what they called "rabbit," you'd live a long time, but the crew would make fun of your high stress, fast moves and quick reflexes. As a coal miner becomes used to the environment, they tend to get a little too comfortable with the noises they hear and the shakes and rattles of the earth. A friend of mine spent his whole life underground. He was a face boss with no rabbit left. Bounces were common in coal mining and you had to have a lot of "rabbit" in those situations. You needed to be quick on your feet. A bounce is a seismic jolt that can cause overhead rock collapses within a coal mine. One day, there was a bounce... several people yelled. Instead of jumping out of harm's way, my friend turned around to look. A large chunk of rock and dirt let loose and crushed him. After bouncing and several people yelling, a new guy with a lot of rabbit would've been down the crosscut, past the kitchen and on his way home!

Many things happened in the two and a half years in Emery County... A few injuries at work, some down time with strikes, many happy times at Joe's Valley Reservoir, some great friends and neighbors, a lot of driving to visit family on weekends, etc. Castle Dale is also where that missionary from my youth ended up living and it was nice to live close to him and get to know his family. There's nothing that will ever replace the magic of my favorite missionary, the Detective!

Before I leave this treasured memory of Emery County, one of the greatest pieces of wisdom from a Mormon bishop to a young married man there was this: "Paul, I'm a banker and a lot of people come in and they want to buy a car, so I'm always financing cars. When I look upon you and your sweet wife, I see that your devoted love for her is as a solid brick.

And that's what I look at when I give a loan to an individual, their credit history. They're solid like a brick as your love for Karen." *My ego was totally getting pumped.* "Now look at your sweet wife. Isn't she just a beautiful flower? What does a brick due to a flower? It'll crush it! Always treat a flower with the kind of care that a kind gardener with great foresight would treat a delicate flower!" Very wise words, that I would refer back to often.

Back in those early days we did not have TiVo and we could not pause the live television shows that played. We had no recorded television shows. I knew, of course, that communication was important to a young couple, but talking during the segment of M.A.S.H. would interrupt Hawkeyes' wit and funny humor and if you missed the joke you might as well just shut off the television. My bit of husbandly wisdom? Shut the TV down and communicate with your spouse! If you're really focused on entertainment that's all you'll have in the long run. No television show is more important than your spouse!

I've been richly rewarded by living with greater interest in my wife than in entertainment or other pursuits. I wonder what would've happened if that wisdom imparted to me by that bishop had not ever been spoken out loud to me. In my mind, my love for Karen was a brick, so solid that she never had to worry about it. Therefore, she never had to hear me tell her how pretty she is and how much I favor being with her, or how I love the color of her eyes, the smell of her hair, etc. And that silent brick would've killed her and my relationship would've been over a long time ago. I'm grateful to a wise bishop who knows about financing and bricks, but especially flowers!

Alas, the Coal Industry changed and I, along with many others, got laid off. It was now time to move back to the big city of Provo to launch Brennan Trucking...

Paul Joseph Brennan

Chapter 9

Brennan Trucking and Excavation

We lost a $14.72 an hour paycheck, as well as our company benefits, when the coal mines laid us off due to a shutdown. Back then that was a good paycheck! Back in the "Big city" of Provo, Utah, we had a little savings and our overhead was low because we only had to pay Park rent for our mobile home. I did have to hit the ground running though, because Karen was pregnant with Jessica Rae.

I had my eye on a dump truck that I had passed by a few times. I saw this truck and asked the owner if he would allow me to purchase the vehicle with the money I could generate. He consented to give me time to make payments as I worked. After getting it in working order and licensed, insured and put on a job site, I would then pay him the asking price. It was an old B model Mack.

I remember the first load coming out of the yard and the highway patrolman shaking his head.

"This is a pit truck, you're overweight before you even get a load on it. I'm not going to give you a ticket, but I am going to tell you to go buy a different truck."

My heart was broken, but it didn't stop me. I found another truck! It was going to take a co-signer for a loan, though. My father-in-law pulled me aside and requested that I let him help finance the truck. He recognized my hard work providing for my family, after hustling two jobs at a time, then working hard in the coal mines and resurrecting a pit truck. It was nice to have someone other than myself and my sweet wife believe in me enough to put their name on the line.

Brennan Trucking had a humble beginning, many ups and downs, but unfortunately it didn't last. There were several accidents and winter shutdowns that took their toll on our struggling new business. Despite Brennan Trucking only lasting five years, I will always value the faith my father in law had I me. And though my experiences were sometimes difficult, there are a few memories that deserve to be remembered.

Down by the water treatment plant in Orem, next to Utah Lake, there was a pile of very dark, black rich earth. It was the cleanup waste from the overflow and the re-building of new silos for the wastewater treatment plant. No wonder why the dirt was so rich and black! It came from the south end of everyone who lived in Utah County. I struck a deal with the city of Orem. I would get rid of that long heaped up length of waste, free of charge! They came back and made a counter-offer of a one-dollar per yard. Sold!

I then turned around and sold the soil for $15 a yard! I had 100,000 yards of human poop filled soil! The city of Orem was building a brand-new hospital, which required a huge amount of topsoil. They wanted the black kind, not the hard pan sand everybody else had. So, I worked out a deal with the hospital to trade them my topsoil in exchange for my bill for the delivery of my daughter Jessica Rae. They agreed.

I am just so amazed at how easy this life can be and what people can use for barter. A gem so precious as my Jessica Rae! And they traded me for their own poop. Think about it, it's really funny! What took them years to poop out and pile up, and they are now paying me to load it into a truck and bring it back and have it spread out for them to grow grass! Not only did I trade the hospital for my bill for the birth of Jessica, I also made about $10,000.00 that summer on that dark, rich dirt!

In working with the landscapers, I got a nickname for myself. All the Spanish landscapers called me "Rocketman". In the world of independent truckers, we help each other find jobs. A friend of mine, a big guy named "Tiny", wanted to help deliver my rich black soil to customers. He would load his own truck when I was out on a delivery at the time he needed to get loaded. I told him, "Just don't take anything out of this specific pile, because I cleaned the road and just piled it up there. We don't use what floats and is not biodegradable from women's hygiene." *They look like little plastic rockets!*

Returning from a delivery, I saw that the loader was parked in the "do not load" pile! By the time I could get in touch with my friend, he had already dumped a load of it and the landscape crew had spread it out on the most deserving pious, snooty brat on the River Bottoms of Provo. This lady came out of her multimillion-dollar home and saw that her entire yard was covered with little white rockets surrounded by very black earth! She started shrieking at the landscape crew, demanding to know what those things were.

Victor, the Spanish landscaper, said, "Lady if you don't know what they are, I don't want to tell you!"

Of course, they both knew very well what they were, because it was very obvious and there were just so many of them all over her yard!

The owner of the landscape company called my wife and was very angry. In the middle of trying to be vocal and angry, he burst out laughing uncontrollably. My wife was also laughing. When she called me and told me that I was in trouble, she could not stop laughing! By the time I got back in touch with the crew, I had already been dubbed "Rocketman"!

The next morning very early, my friend Tiny and I showed up with two 5-gallon buckets and a rake and we hooked and raked and dumped them all in our buckets, until they were both full, and then we got the heck out of there! And, by the way, in case you were wondering, that rich black earth was safe from any bacteria or contamination. It was tested from a lab and it had been in the sun long enough to be bacteria free!

In the construction industry, you always get a nickname. I was very grateful for "Rocket man" because the one that preceded that was "Crash"! I know you've got in your mind something terrible, but really it was pretty funny...

It was early morning, in the winter on the lakefront, and fog was always a problem before the sun came up. I was at a T intersection with no time to slow down and make a proper turn. I hit the brakes, turned the wheel, and slid sideward right through the intersection into a farmer's field, where I broadsided an abandoned chicken coop. Splinters everywhere! Feathers everywhere! I wished it could've been on video. I spent half the day that next Saturday with the fence post digger cleaning up all the boards, splinters and Playboy magazines that were all over. I did that farmer a favor that day and took away his nephew's excuse to dis appear from his chores. I bet a lot got done after that chicken coop got smashed into itsy-bitsy chicken nuggets.

Three guys die. Two of them were preachers and one of them was a bus driver. The two preachers were enjoying their walk through the silver clouds of eternity when, on their return, they found something very disturbing. It looked to be much nicer than both of their inheritances put together. The beautiful scenery attached to this property, the fountains and rolling hillsides as far as the eye could see off in the distance and the most brilliant white rock presidential wall surrounding a white marble castle! Surely this estate belongs to Peter! But when they came to the entrance of the circular drive with fountains and quarter horses trotting about, they read the nameplate and it was addressed to the bus driver!

This was so emotionally overwhelming for the two preachers who spent their entire lives building the kingdom of God and getting much less of an inheritance than a mere bus driver, they had to bring it to the attention of Peter and get an answer, now! Peter met them, and trying to calm them down and assure them that all is fair in heaven, he said, "You see, it's real simple feller's... that one bus driver made more people pray than both you boys put together!"

The winters in the mountains along the Wasatch front are frozen, cold and miserable! For an excavation trucking business, you can't really haul frozen earth anywhere. Well not entirely true, as I did have a winter job my last year in business hauling wet mud to Salt Lake City. It's not something I recommend though.

On one trip, my brother David, who was home on leave from the Marines, was riding with me. While dumping this load, one third of it stuck to the top right-hand corner of the dump bed and it caused the truck to slowly tip over. While it was descending to the ground, my brother David was inquiring as to what was going on and I calmly informed him that the truck was tipping over. Very calm, but very obvious, as to what was happening then, we were both holding on and moving our feet as it went over.

We were basically standing on the passenger door when it was all said and done. As the front end weighed about as much as the load of frozen mud, the truck took its time in the descent and ended up twisted in half! The insurance agent was an angel and helped in the recovery of our now useless truck, but it took about 90 days to get it welded back together and fish plated. However, there was not enough money for all the downtime, shop time, parts and labor.

While putting my lifeblood into the recovery of the truck, I received a phone call from my wife with tears and trepidation. Our little Jessica was facing eminent danger. At any given moment, her airway could stop her from breathing and she could die! Jessica was just two years old and had just swallowed two pennies. They were lodged in her throat and when the doctors would try to retrieve them they would act as tweezers and pinch onto the tissue lining of her throat! Karen's plead to me was to use my priesthood authority and ask for a miracle that the doctors would be able to get these pennies dislodged without surgery yet still save our baby's life!

When I hung up the phone, I was in the deepest rut of despair. My life was weighed and measured against what was most important and wonderful in my life. It was my treasure at the other end of that phone and it seemed as though it could be taken away from me at any time. My greatest joy in life is to be a husband and a father. Now the stress of being the owner of something that was sucking the life out of me to make a living, while my baby might be dying, was almost more than I could handle.

I offered up a heartfelt prayer that day. A desperate plea of a father begging for the life of his child. Then in a moment that I'll never forget, as soon as I said "Amen", the phone rang and I was alerted that the pennies were no longer a threat! Hmmmm…. Miracle? Yes! I know my Heavenly Father watches over every wrench that's turned, and every penny that's picked up or stepped over or accidentally swallowed by an 18-month old child. I love my Heavenly Father and his son Jesus Christ! And most especially, his gift of the Holy Ghost to buoy up the haggard soul of a truck driver turned mechanic.

As I mentioned previously, Brennon Trucking wouldn't last. After losing what felt like my soul in chapter 13 bankruptcy, my little family and I moved into the basement of my father in law's home. My in-laws were very kind and loving and never held our circumstances against me, but I was holding those things against myself. We are almost always our own worst critic! Karen was very hormonal and emotional. There was an enormous amount of stress we attributed it to, but then we found out she was also miscarrying a pregnancy that was still unbeknownst to us at the time. These experiences, followed by a car accident that injured my back and put me out of commission for a while, sealed the deal of being the lowest and hardest point in our lives, thus far. We began pushing each other away, instead of drawing closer together in the trials.

We didn't stay with Karen's parents for very long, though it seemed like forever, but it was one of the most difficult places to be emotionally. As a man, I've always taken the roll of provider very seriously. And, at this time in my life, I felt like a complete failure. This point in our marriage was the closest we ever came to allowing the stresses of life to break us apart. We had to decide that, with everything we had lost, we were not going to lose each other! Everything that we had lost so far was not as valuable as our marriage and our growing family. We just needed to get back on our feet and move on with life.

Just before the car accident I mentioned had happened, we were already wanting an escape from our circumstances in life. We felt a change of job and scenery might be just what was needed, so I applied for a job in southern California at an amazing nursery in a gorgeous section of San Juan Capistrano. The job would even include living right on the nursery property. We could just picture raising our girls there! It seemed all our troubles would just melt away if we got this job. But as with every big decision we make, we prayed to find out if it was the correct decision for our family. We wanted so badly for the answer to be "Yes". I knew God would steer us in the right direction, so I prayed that, if it was the right course for us, my starting pay rate would not be less than a certain amount. We didn't need a lot, just enough that we wouldn't have to worry about paying the rent.

A short time later, I received a phone call informing me that I got the job and they wanted me to start as soon as I could make it down there. Only one problem... they would start me fifty cents lower than I had mentioned in my prayer to God. Even though this was the verification I had requested in my prayer to help me know if we should not take the job, I rationalized it away because they had also mentioned they would increase my pay later if I did well. With that in mind, we headed down to California! We were so intent on going that I didn't even call the employer to let them know I would accept the job. Our journey didn't last long though. It ended abruptly with a head-on collision!

Our first concern was for our girls who were in the back seat of the car. With God's mercy they were fine, as was Karen. I, however, was not! The impact of my head hitting the windshield and my chest hitting the steering wheel severely injured my back and I was in major pain. Needless to say, with the accident and my injury, I didn't even remember to call the nursery in California to let them know I wanted to take the job and it was given to someone else. Of course, it wouldn't really have mattered anyway, as I ended up out of commission for quite some time later and was unable to work. *Seriously, hadn't we been through enough?*

Looking back now, we both feel that a caring Heavenly Father did not want us to take that job for certain reasons we will never know in this Earth life. Because we had disregarded the answer and sign I had been given, he helped us to not make a life changing mistake! I recovered from my injuries with time and, even though we were very disappointed at times with not being able to follow the dreams and plans we had made, we felt gratitude that our Heavenly Father knows more than we do, and that he is watching over us. Some may say that it was just an accident, but we feel in our hearts that it was no accident. It was divine intervention.

Sometime later, when my back had healed enough, I became a bus driver with a charter company who served the Wasatch Front. Part of my job was to get contracts with high schools for our company to provide transportation for their school choir trips out of town. It was fun working with the high school choirs because they were always going to the coolest places. And they always wanted me to be the driver!

One of my favorite trips was when we took a High School group to Disneyland. Actually, *they* flew and I deadheaded out with a mostly empty bus. Empty, except for my wife and daughters, who were allowed to come with me on this trip. The choir didn't realize I would be the one driving the bus around until they saw us cheering their excellent performances. After that, they wanted us to hang with them and thus we had 27 babysitters. There was only one problem with having your small giggly daughters on a bus with 27 teenagers. The girls ended up thinking that flagellating on the laps of the choir members was funny. Every time they did it, the entire bus would laugh hysterically and that was pouring gas on the fire. *Pun intended.* So, getting them to quit was pretty much impossible. Thus, a new game began. It was: *Pass the kid until it farts... you win!*

It can be a little difficult traveling with children. Especially when late nights are planned and there is a bedtime involved. One of the planned evening dinners was at a theme restaurant that had a dance stage. Karen stayed at the hotel with Tiffany and Jessica because this was going to end up being a late return dinner. The servers at the restaurant were required to dress up as the actor they thought they looked most like. If they were just dirt ugly, they'd have to be an obvious cartoon character! Not a problem, except for one of the waitresses was dressed up as an old time western saloon waitress with fishnet pantyhose and voluptuous bosoms! Of course, all the young men wanted to hang out with her and get pictures. They figured they'd put me up to it first, but there was no way I wanted this picture getting back to my wife. I didn't want to take the picture!

I've always felt it's easier to not have to explain anything, just don't do it in the first place! But these boys were thespians. Mix that with a restaurant full of actresses and waiters and it was pretty crazy! So, the waitress got real cheesy and put her leg up in my arm and when I got very close... of course, everyone took pictures! I made them promise these pictures would never show up on the bus with my family. I did not want to have any negativity or demand for divorce papers to be signed. They agreed, and it worked out just fine. Nobody showed my wife any pictures, but these kids had such a fun time with us that when we returned home, they all wanted to meet us at a restaurant in Salt Lake City the next week. On Wednesdays, I was the tour guide at Temple Square. So, after my shift, my wife and I were met at the restaurant by a half dozen of those choir teenagers. I was thrilled to see them, but very surprised to see the pictures they were sharing!

I had thought I was out of the woods... Nope! Needless to say, my wife had some questions about what had taken place that night at the restaurant in California. I was innocent, but appeared very guilty! Luckily, I'm a trustworthy guy, so all was well. If I had ever given her a reason to doubt earlier on in our marriage, I'd have been in trouble! Keep your integrity intact at all times. It will serve you well, especially with your spouse. Don't ever give them any reason for doubt. It's not in your best interest, or theirs. Trust is an important thing in a marriage, or in any relationship for that matter.

Life is full of lessons. Isn't that why we're here anyway? We can get ourselves into all kinds of trouble by our actions.

It's important to always keep our honor and stay on the right side of things. It's hard to earn back trust once it's lost. Why not keep the trust there in the first place?

Though my time as a bus driver was memorable and quite enjoyable, my career was not to end up there. There was a furniture company, back in the day of waterbeds, that made waterbed headboards of every size that you could imagine. They also made hutches with mirrors and nightstands, all with the same look and all very heavy! They sold to 48 states and had coast-to-coast delivery. I worked for them for a while delivering their wood furniture. I would have to load and unload my own tractor-trailer with all that heavy stuff! I delivered it all over the country. In fact, I was gone more than I was home during that time in our lives. It was hard leaving my family. My girls were still very young and, of course, back then there were no cell phones. Communication was difficult.

On one occasion, I found myself looking for a phone booth to make a call home; not a regular scheduled call, but one that you just get that deep down bluesy, I'm missing my family, kind of feeling. Have you ever tried to find a parking place in downtown Chicago that could fit 80 feet of vehicle, just to use a phone booth? By the time it worked out and I got Karen on the phone, she was amazed at my call, specifically the very moment of my call. She wasn't expecting it until the next day or night. I really was not big on calling often, so we had a call schedule. I was big on getting the job done and getting home.

Tiffany, our oldest daughter, was about 3 years old or so and was learning how to put sentences together in a very limited vocabulary. Though limited, it was very animated! In her cute, deep voice, she would say, "In'a talk to Daddy." Karen would tell her that I would call sometime the next day, as I usually called every few days when I was gone for two weeks. One night, Tiffany asked her Heavenly Father through prayer to help her Daddy call her to say "Good Night". While she was praying, Karen, being a very good mom, was trying to figure out a nice way to let her know that sometimes prayers take a while to get answered, and we don't always get them answered the way we wish. She didn't want her to be disappointed when I didn't call. She was worried that her little girls wouldn't understand about how prayers work.

As little Tiffany ended her prayer, (in her words) "the phone dinged" and a very happy yet surprised mother answered the phone and told me I had to speak to Tiffany right away! She handed the phone to my daughter, who said "Daddy, In'a hold you!" I felt like leaving that rig right where it was and giving up trucking forever!

This same little girl, in one of her morning prayers, asked Heavenly Father on a clear sunny day if he would send her a rainbow so she could take a picture of it. Karen again tried to explain to her that sometimes prayers take a while to get answered and it might take a while longer than that day. Karen saw that there were no clouds in sight and she didn't even have film in the camera, so she knew there was no way there would be any pictures of rainbows that day.

Tiffany shrugged it off like, "Yeah, whatever." and went back to playing. Karen was thinking that she'd buy some film and get the camera ready for a future rainbow. Well, later that afternoon, they walked up the hill to visit grandma at her home overlooking Lions Park in Provo, across the valley from BYU and the Provo Temple. At grandma's house, they were watching TV and just taking it easy when grandma yelled from the kitchen window to come see something pretty.

They ran to see what she was talking about and right there out the window was a neon double rainbow that went completely across the sky and ended at the Provo Temple. Karen immediately started crying! Little Tiffy was standing against the back of the couch pointing out the big picture window saying, "Look mom, my rainbow!" Karen could not believe it! She asked her mother if she film in her camera.

Alice said, "Yes, I just put a new roll in today."

Why do we doubt God's goodness and ability to perform large, or small, miracles? My girls were so full of faith and hope and make-believe; they were princesses. They were smart too! They always knew where we were headed, like trying to surprise them by taking them swimming or camping. I mean it wasn't even a question. They would always figure it out. We could never surprise them! But they were always so excited when "Daddy's home", when the big truck would back into the driveway! You'd think "the Care Bears" or "Big Bird" was in there with me!

They were always jumping up-and-down, clapping and yelling, "Daddy's home! Daddy's home!" And then the "cab lizard" would come down out of his big rig and grab them both up and give them a "raspberry" on their bellies! And then there were "giggle monster" wrestling matches! And even though we were heading to bankruptcy, I never wanted my children to go through what I went through. So, I tried so hard to pretend everything was so happy and fun! Of course, it was for them, but it had to be a miserable nightmare for poor Karen.

Her dad had worked 40 years at the Steel mill and never skipped a payday and now we never knew when one was coming, except when the truck was running. And the stress from catching up on back payments and tires and fuel and no cell phones. It was tough, looking back! It would have helped so much for her to be able to communicate with me on an adult level during the days of depression and stress. But our girls had a good childhood. They knew none of the stress and fear that I had gone through on a daily basis as a child. They had parents that loved each other. They had fun and giggles and happiness. They had hope and prayers and miracles and music. Even in times of sadness, stress, and trouble, they still knew love and happiness and hope.

We need to protect our children. They trust us, and they depend on us. Who else can they turn to if they can't turn to their parents? Raising a family under the influence of the restored Gospel of Jesus Christ beats the heck out of raising a family under the influence of alcohol! I know this from experience. We were plagued with similar butt-kicking life challenges that my parents went through and yet, with the fundamental lessons taught every Sunday, we had the wisdom of living prophets and apostles to help us through it all.

Chapter 10

Devil's Playground

My jobs were always tough, but interesting! If you keep your heart open, you can find life lessons and things to smile about in each challenge you face. I spent a summer with a cab over a tractor lowboy trailer, gathering railroad ties out of the desert. I would then deliver them all up and down the California Coast for landscape companies and stores.

One day, after an overnight stay in a hotel in the middle of nowhere, I went down into Devils Playground without any water or provisions. It was to be a simple quick trip, just like many others. Except this time the crew had moved and I missed the turn when going to the new location. In the desert, it's all dirt roads. So, when I hurried to make a wide turn, the sand grabbed the tandems on my truck and I was stuck! I tried to dig myself out, but it was useless.

I would dig for 10-15 minutes, then drive and only move half a foot. I needed to travel 30 yards! Thirty yards is not that far, but at a half a foot per 20 minutes, I was exhausted to say the least. Looking up at the sun, I realized I had no water. I was very thirsty and figured I was going to die. It was about 115 degrees out! When I thought about this, I could actually imagine hearing Rod Serling talking about the Twilight Zone and a young man entering the desert never to leave again. Of course, I could not just stop trying, but my efforts were slowing down quite a bit. As I had an occasional view of the horizon waving in the heat, in my imagination I kept hearing that sound of the Twilight Zone mingled with some old western music and even the soundtrack of "The Good, The Bad and The Ugly."

Did I mention that I have a high disregard for snakes? Well, I do! And in this desert, they seem to weigh 40 or 50 pounds when they slap their body on the earth and their other half is in the air and they look like a corkscrew in fast motion, going across the road. The sidewinders just made me put all my emotions into the paddle on that diesel rig, as if it had some magic power of crushing them. Then come those delusional, heat induced thoughts... *The snakes are not crushed. They're wrapped up in my axle. As soon as I get out, they're going to wrap around me!*

Did I say I was thirsty? I was *really* thirsty! So, what do you do when there's no water, you're really thirsty, you're surrounded by snakes, and you've only moved 6 feet in the past two hours? Oh yeah, I'm pretty sure I mentioned it was 115 degrees of blasting sun out there! I'll tell you what you do. You pray, because praying is the only thing left before you die! Sometimes in these situations, your prayers are comical because they are your last thoughts and they are under duress. You're also speaking out loud and nobody is around. You might mention a few idiot things that you did to cause your own demise, like simply buying a gallon of water before you go out into the desert in the hot summer.

No matter how inconvenient it is, GO get some water and then go into the desert, just in case it ends up being no simple trip in and out like you've done so many other times. The crew gathering railroad ties is about 8 miles away and the hotel that you stayed in is about 20 miles back. Either way, you're dead because you don't have any energy left. And you say your faithful prayer, knowing it's your last prayer and the words spoken fall only upon your own ears... you think...

The word *Amen* came with a small blue speck in the wavy

heat of the horizon. Further staring, the blue speck gets bigger… what else are you going to do but keep staring as the blue speck turns into a vehicle, that turns into a Subaru, that turns into a grandpa with a grandson/boy scout who stops 10 feet away from you and asks, "Do you need any help?"

Well, in my head I'm thinking, "Of course, I do!" but from my lips nothing came. All I could do was stare at him in amazement that the word *Amen* makes a blue speck turn into a grandpa and a boy scout in a Subaru! This would make a great Subaru commercial. The best word I could come up with in my amazed, stunned and very thirsty state of mind was "water". But it didn't sound like water, it sounded more like "Waaa", in a hoarse whisper. This kind man got out of his vehicle and opened the back hatch. I saw the most beautiful, gorgeous, orange, Gott cooler. You know, the ones with the white top, 5-gallon size. Just enough for me!

I don't know what those guys were going to drink after that, but I just wanted to climb inside of that jug and absorb it through my tongue! I just wanted that water to be a part of me. I was so in need of water! Well, after about seven of those paper cups of water, I was able to answer one of their questions. Then I asked them one question in return… "What brings you out into the desert, today of all days?"

Grandpa says, "I haven't been out here for 20 years! I just thought my grandson needed to learn a little bit about desert life. He's a Boy Scout, you know, and they need to learn about all different kinds of life."

I was grateful for that grandpa teaching his young grandson about life in the desert, especially on that day. And most especially at the end of a prayer that I knew, for sure, was going to be my last. I knew I was going to go to sleep and never wake up, but they saved my life. I'm beholden to grandpas, boy scouts, Subaru's and Gott coolers, and water… but most especially, I am grateful to know a wise and loving Heavenly

Father inspires grandpas to take grandsons out into the desert in a timely manner to help a poor, desperate guy like me stay a few moments longer on this planet. I'd grown very accustomed to this earth life and I very much love all of God's creations, but... did I tell you I hate snakes?!

Some might say that this was a coincidence! I call it a miracle! Ordinary or not, it was another miracle in my life that has granted me more days to hang out on this planet called Earth and watch my kids and grandkids grow and become amazing human beings.

Chapter 11

Darkened Abyss and Despair

This guy died and Peter was showing him how beautiful celestial glory is. Peter was running short on time for another meeting and asked if they could please reunite after lunch to finish his introduction to celestial glory. The man thanked Peter, but he was puzzled and asked why Heaven had lines to stand in for lunch? Peter laughed and said, "The food is worth the wait. I'll meet you right here after lunch." And off he went.

The new saint in line was rudely bumped by an elbow pushing him out of line. Someone cut in front of him and everyone else all the way to the front of the line. This man grabbed his lunch and stormed off to eat it elsewhere! The new saint was taken aback to the point almost of anger, but quickly he turned it to a high level of concern. He knew that he could find out from Peter why someone as rude as this could be in such a nice place.

While eating, the food was so good that he almost forgot completely about the incident. But when they continued their tour after lunch, and after explaining how rude this person was that had elbowed everyone in line and rushed off, Peter interrupted him and asked, "Was he about yay tall and dressed all in green?"

"Why yes how did you know?"

"Oh," smiled Peter… "That was God pretending to be a doctor!"

Another pregnancy. By the time Karen told me she thought she was pregnant, I already knew. Through divine inspiration, I also knew she was having twins. I didn't know if they were boys or girls, or one of each, but I knew they were twins!

We were excited about Karen's pregnancy, especially about it being twins, but early on Karen didn't feel right. She felt like something was wrong. Her doctor assured her that carrying twins felt different, but that he was sure everything was fine. She kept trying to tell him this was not just a normal twin thing but that something was not right. Finally, an ultrasound was ordered and the doctor informed us that there *was* a problem called "twin to twin transfusion". This is where one baby doesn't get enough amniotic fluid, as well as other nutrients, and the other baby gets too much.

The doctors ordered Karen on bed rest and instructed her to lay on her left side as much as possible. Not an easy thing when you have two small energetic girls that need a lot of attention every day, but if it could help the babies then it would be worth it. Karen had a lot of pain that nothing would alleviate, so this made it easier to stay down. Even with that, things got worse. When things didn't improve, another ultrasound was done that showed things were going to get worse before they got better.

They gave us three choices...

First choice: Do nothing and most likely miscarry both babies.

Second choice: Stay at the local hospital near our home and be on medication to try stopping an early labor. Then, hope for the best if the babies came early, which most likely they would anyway.

Third choice: Travel by ambulance to the LDS Hospital in North Salt Lake City, almost two hours away from home and our girls, and they would try to stop labor. If the babies did come early, they had an experimental drug called Surfactant, a medication known to help a baby's premature lungs keep from collapsing. This would give them a little better chance at surviving so early on.

We made the only choice that made sense to us. We would do anything that might give the babies the best chance at life! Karen was rushed by ambulance to the LDS Hospital in Salt Lake City. Our emotions were bordering between fear and stress. At this point, we knew that the twins were not big enough or developed enough to have much of a chance to live outside of the womb. The doctors were hoping for the best-case scenario of Karen staying down and nothing happening for as long as possible.

So, with trepidation and hope in our hearts, we had to leave our two girls, Tiffany and Jessica, home with Karen's parents. This was very difficult because we knew we could end up being at the hospital for a few months. Three of the hospital's top surgeons were planning the best way to save the precious lives of my wife and our twins when delivery was imminent. They would be ready with three surgical teams, one for Karen and the C-section and one for each twin. After 10 days, Karen's temperature shot up! The doctors said there was some kind of infection that could kill her and the babies if she didn't deliver them STAT. We were only at 25 weeks, most definitely too soon for the babies to survive.

I don't recall much about eating food all the days prior to the surgery. I know I was fasting and praying. I know we had given her many blessings. And I know that our daughters were with their grandma and grandma, Gene and Alice Campbell. I know my daughters needed support and love from their daddy...their happy daddy! The one with the Tinker Bell dust! But all the talk from the doctors was so bleak, it was difficult to be the happy daddy. But I also know we were at the best place for the best chance for the twins to survive this premature delivery.

A delivery, by the way, that my insurance company said they would not cover because they were treating it as a pre-existing condition. This had all happened so fast that they figured we were trying to be fraudulent to get them to pay. Knowing the medical bills would be tripled when the babies were born, now with the possibly of no insurance, and the risk of losing my wife and the twins, reality was really starting to weigh on my spirit! Karen didn't know anything about the insurance call until much later. I would protect her from the reality as long as possible.

Katrina was born first, and a team of doctors huddled around Karen broke from the center to their own corner. Shortly after this, Kassandra was taken with her team of doctors to her corner. I was left with Karen in the middle; her sweet face was looking up at me with a beautiful smile. There was a blue curtain that separated her view from the reality of what was happening, but not mine... They had given her an epidural but kept her fully awake because they assumed this would be her only chance to see the babies alive.

I did my best to be a strength for my amazing wife. I would look at her with the tender love I felt for her, then I would look below the blue tarp and see her guts all heaped up just below her rib cage and an amazing amount of blood as they were putting her back together again. All the while I was holding her hand trying to comfort her, I was determined to keep my cool. It was very trying, to say the least.

After letting Karen take a quick peak at the babies, they took her to another room for recovery. The babies had to be taken across town to the University Hospital for their care, I think because the neonatal unit at the LDS hospital was too full right then. This was very difficult for me, hurrying back and forth through town to see my babies and back to Karen. Neither Karen or the babies were doing well. The babies never really stabilized. Doctors kept poking holes in their lungs and filling them with the Surfactant. They had tubes and wires and hoses hooked up everywhere. They each only weighed about a pound and a half.

I know those doctors tried and tried, but Katrina didn't make it. The doctors continued working on Kassandra another 5 ½ hours, through that day and into the night. I was watching her fight and struggle when I knew inside that she wasn't supposed to stay here. I asked for my baby girl, so I could hold her. I kissed her little face and tried to be strong, as I cherished those moments with her until she went back to Heaven to be with her sister and other loved family members who were, no doubt, there to greet her. No more needles, no more gloves, no nursery rhymes or songs, no pixie dust or fairytale songs, no daddy giggly raspberries on their bellies.

Before they died, a name and a blessing was given to these two daughters of Paul Joseph & Karen Sue Brennan, to be known upon the records of the church throughout the moments of their mortality. While they were in the neonatal unit, they were labeled "baby A" and "baby B". That seemed too cold and impersonal, so I relabeled their little incubators with "Sugarplum" and "Sweetpea"! The doctors and nurses liked that and started referring to them by those names. When they received their names and blessings, Katrina was named Katrina Sweetpea Brennan and Kassandra was named Kassandra Sugarplum Brennan. It only seemed right that they would recognize those names that they were called their short time here on earth and I wanted them to keep those names forever.

I can't express how glad I was to have become a practicing Latter Day Saint. Had I stayed a Catholic, I would still be under the assumption that those two beautiful baby girls, dying before they could get baptized, would be condemned to live in an eternal hell with no mercy. That is what was taught to me when I was an altar boy. And my parents would still be doomed to hell because they divorced each other. Who would ever want to believe this? Life sucks enough. Who needs that extra luggage just to weigh you down, or kick your teeth out so you have to get them wired shut and drink through a straw like my brother Bobby? No, I would much rather believe as I do now.

Because I now hold the Priesthood of God, I could give my daughters a name and a blessing upon their departure from this earth. They, being pure without sin, born to loving parents, and leaving after only moments or hours of breath and multiple surgeries (with no anesthetics) would dwell with our Father in Heaven until we meet up with them someday and unite as a forever family. They, as do all others who died before the age of accountability, inherit the highest degree of the Celestial Kingdom and dwell with God and Christ! They become our champions, cheering us on to continue keeping our covenants, pure and undefiled from sin, which is so prevalent in this life. They were perfect little spirits that received their bodies and are waiting for us in Heaven. They will always be a part of our family, for eternity.

When I told Karen that the babies had died, she was on morphine. All she said was, "That's sad." I wanted morphine, because at that point we had slipped into the deepest part of the abyss. The doctors couldn't figure out why Karen wasn't responding to all of the antibiotics and other treatments for the infection and she was suddenly dying as well! The doctors demanded we do an emergency hysterectomy to save her life. STAT! That means quick like a bunny rabbit!

I wouldn't allow the surgery without a reasonable explanation why it had to be done and/or a third-party opinion.

There were three of them and one of me and they said, "Here is your third-party opinion... there's three of us."

I said, "No, you all work together! I want a third-party opinion from someone who doesn't work right in here with you guys, to help figure out a way that she can keep her plumbing and her life! All you guys are telling me is that she's going to die if you don't take her organs for childbearing out."

To be perfectly honest, I was scared stiff to even think about ever having another baby after this, but I just didn't understand. They didn't seem to have the answers I needed to feel good about it. They were always questioning me about my ability to come up with these questions because I sounded like a medical person when I was just a truck driver. You see... I was a prayerful truck driver. I'd been fasting and praying in hopes that the right procedure would be done and in hopes that I would understand the right procedure when it was presented. I wanted an option that would not make me feel as though I were standing next to a war victim blown apart on the surgery table, as I saw my Karen just a few days ago!

The doctors were trying to sway my decision by having the nurse on each shift talk me into saving her life by letting them do the hysterectomy. Karen's mom and dad were upset at me for not letting the doctors do their job on their daughter. I felt at times I had nowhere to turn. I had no insurance to pay for all this, according to the insurance office and the phone call that I had received at the onset of all of this. I felt like I had no allies, except for a friend who had just started a new company called NuSkin International. He and some of his co-workers had taken their commission checks in those early days of being in business, and donated it to Paul and Karen Brennan and they called it "a Paul Grant".

It was very cool to open that check in the presence of Karen's mom and dad who were somewhat wroth with me. I think they felt that I was not giving the doctors a chance to save their daughter's life. I can't blame them for feeling that way, they were afraid. But the more they pushed and insisted using Karen's life as the trump card, it would push me further away from them, all of them. I felt somewhat alone, but I knew that I was being directed by my Heavenly Father to protect our family. I was being guided in what I was supposed to say and do and, even though I was discouraged and alone, I was getting help from guardian angels.

The hospital Karen was in is a training hospital, so all the interns follow their medical trainers and they all wanted to come into the room where my wife's stomach was distended and bloated. She was on morphine; her system was not functioning properly and she was dying. The doctors would push on her stomach and talk to her about how she felt. Then the students would take a turn and push on her stomach… that is, until I put an end to that BS! It looked like the kids (interns) were trying to push her stomach hard enough to make her system kick in. Now none of them liked me, because they couldn't "practice" on her anymore.

There was a head nurse though who looked past her feelings and provided me with much needed food and drink, but most of all, out of the blue, a hug. I almost fainted! I felt my knees start to buckle and could not believe that was actually happening. Compassionate service, or the lack of it, is why my mom became a nurse. Although I know this is not always the case, but she saw how horrible the nursing program was that took care of her son's (my brother) last living days on earth. So she went to school to become a nurse and improve the field, which she did with levity and love!

Some of the doctors that were under such great stress and did not, or could not, show their compassion would be grounded by my mom. She would just smile while adjusting her reading glasses with her middle finger, flipping them off right to their faces, earning a gasp! *"Mary how rude, but really funny!"* These were all honorable and good men, most of them holding high positions in the Church of Jesus Christ of Latter Day Saints (Mormons). Yeah, Mary was pretty gutsy! And she always seemed to get away with it.

True story... Two men were in Mary's care at the hospital, alcoholics in recovery. Both of them were LDS, both of them in temple garments; one of them had horrible hygiene and was very open about his addiction, the other with impeccable hygiene and very good at hiding his addiction while keeping his business and his church calling in balance. It was bound to catch up with the latter at some point, but so far hadn't. Nurse Mary burst into their shared room at the hospital and told them both, "I have good news and bad news. What do you want to hear first?" The good news... "OK you're both getting a change of underwear! The bad news, you're swapping with each other!" She did have a great sense of humor.

Because Karen was feeling so awful and sick, I laid down the law that no friends, church or family members could stop by the hospital to visit. George and his family, an awesome Polynesian family that lived right across the street from us, didn't listen. They brought their entire tribe, their ukuleles, their leis, their love and their money and came anyway. They visited. They sang. They were the best neighbors!

George was my home teaching companion at the time. He would rarely visit families with me, but he would send his nephew. His nephew was stateside because of trouble on the islands involving a drug dealer that threatened to shoot him on the count of three. When he got to two, this boy shot first. Simple math. Later on, in Provo, the same thing happened on Center Street. This time a bouncer threatened and so he shot him too!

We happened to visit my friend on occasion, the friend that had given me his commission checks when he found out my insurance wouldn't cover our medical bills. After one visit, my friend asked me if I had any other known killers that I wanted to bring by. Sarcasm noted! But this boy was no cold-hearted killer. I had lived with killers in Boston and I knew the difference. You can sense the difference. I loved this kid. He loved his family. He just needed some counseling and guidance. Heavenly Father uses friends, family and strangers to provide his extended love, called tender mercies and perfect timing. When it came time to bury our twin's, we would again need those tender mercies.

Chapter 12

A Breath of Fresh Air

Karen was still in the hospital not doing well and I had to go take care of the graveside service with my two little girls at my side. Karen's mom stayed with her, two hours away. She still had an unknown infection in her system. No food or water by mouth, tons of antibiotics and a tube down her throat pumping everything out, yet she still wasn't improving. They told us she had blood clots blocking everything in her system. It was difficult leaving her at that time, but it wasn't possible to be two places at once.

Our friend, Patriarch Jesse Clyde Sumsion, spoke at the twin's graveside service. He spoke of how Karen and I, in the pre-earth life, desired so much to have a family together forever, not just "until death do we part". That just makes love stare into darkness! But to be sealed by the power and authority of those holding that power in the holy temples of God, we have the privilege of reuniting after death with all of our loved ones sealed to each other. Sealed to Heavenly Father and Heavenly Mother and to continue on as a family throughout all time and throughout all eternity. We will all be one eternal round.

Everything we do and everything we go through in this earth life is giving us experience that will help us become more like our Heavenly parents. We're on this earth to gain experience through our trials and opposition. It's like a refiner's fire... getting rid of impurities with each trial, depending on how we deal with it. Attitude determines altitude! I can't imagine going through trials without God above me, picking me up and lifting me each time I get knocked down.

One day, a new doctor came into our hospital room and Karen, still being on morphine, thought he was an angel. She felt something good was going to happen. *They should give both husband and wife morphine in times like this!* This doctor told us he had an idea what the problem was with Karen's infection and he had heard we were against the hysterectomy. He told us he felt that a hysterectomy was not needed and explained his idea.

"Does it have anything to do with pulling out all of her female plumbing?" I asked.

"No, not at all," he said. "She'll still be able to have children, as this is a simple procedure and can be done in an office with local anesthetic. It's something to try, before we go to more invasive procedures."

"What are we waiting for, Doc?"

They ordered a clean room, not an operating room. The procedure was performed without records and without video. He opened Karen up and pulled out several bloody things and threw them into the trashcan! Karen's digestive system kicked in that night and we went home the day after that! So, what was all the STAT crap about a hysterectomy or she's going to die? There had been so many people in that surgical room when they were putting Karen back together, the count of gauze was forgotten!

Later, when I told Karen and the doctors that the insurance company canceled the policy because they said it was a pre-existing condition, the doctor that did the C-section offered his services for free if the insurance ended up not paying. Tender mercies! Two amazing doctors and one amazing nurse. Hindsight... I loved and appreciated all those doctors and nurses. All of them. They did their best in trying to save my babies and my wife, but what they put me through because of that mistake was one of the most challenging experiences of my life and had me at odds with the nicest people that I love dearly... Karen's parents.

I could have sued, but where would that have gotten me? Heavenly Father blessed our little family with the possibility of having more children. How could I throw that back in his face by turning the whole thing into another big negative? We knew it would have not been the right thing to do. It would not have brought our baby girls back, nor would it have changed the outcome of any of the experiences we went through. There was no point.

It was amazing to be home again with our two girls! Back to being a family again, even though we were mourning the loss of our baby girls! Tiffany and Jessica had been so excited to have the girls join our family and they were still pretty sad. They would sit out on the sidewalk and watch for someone to walk past with a baby, just so they could catch a glimpse. It was kind of heartbreaking. But we had received another "ordinary miracle" and life began to get back to normal. Except that another move was in the horizon.

This move was different though than previous ones. I had prayed for guidance on all of our other moves. I asked my sweet Karen to fast and pray this time about where we should move. I wanted Karen to feel the pressure and the blessing that comes from fasting and prayer with such a weighty matter. Where will our children attend school? Where will I gain the best employment and have everything else work out as well? Karen promised me that we could sell pencils together and that she'd help if we could just get away from the cold of Utah's winters! So, we both agreed that somewhere around the Nevada border would be great!

Shortly after we started our search, I was on a bus charter

with a group of Salt Lake people at a convention in Anaheim, California, and I was in route to come home when I called Karen. She asked me to stop by a town called Ivins to check out a property that had been offered to her by a friend in our ward in Provo. Karen told me she had been on her knees feeling the weight of responsibility to the future blessings of our family and had decided that she would not rise from her knees until she got an answer as to which town or city we should move to. Not very long after she made this conviction to not get up, the phone rang.

The voice on the other side of the phone was a lady from our neighborhood that neither Karen nor I knew very well. She had heard that we were going to be moving and was calling to let Karen know that she was sad and had been looking forward to getting to know us better and become friends. During the conversation, she mentioned that she had an old mobile home in a small town near St. George, Utah, very close to the border of Nevada. It had recently been occupied by less than responsible people. It had basically been trashed and the yard very neglected. Karen told me about it and asked me to stop by and see how bad it was.

When I saw this humble trailer with weeds that had grown as tall as the trailer itself, I was caught off guard! It was a fire hazard, as well as an eyesore! I felt exactly the way the pioneers who settled the western front must have felt when a wagon wheel would break off the axle of a buckboard.

Agnes looked at her husband Eggbert and asked, "What are we going to do now?" Eggbert gazed westward, northward, southward, and then looked back at that buckboard's broken wheel. Having no spare he said, "( ) this looks good to me"… and that's how Kansas got settled! Speaking of Kansas… that reminds me of a shirt that my kid brother had. It said, "Auntie Em, Hate you! Hate Kansas! Taking the dog, Dorothy!"

Desperate times call for desperate measures though, so we decided it was time for an adventure to Southern Utah! We drove there with all of our belongings loaded into a U-Haul truck, even though Karen had never seen it in person. I actually made the mobile home sound worse than it was to Karen. I figured that if I made it sound really bad, then maybe when she actually saw it, she would be surprised that it was better than she imagined. It worked... until we started working on it and realized that almost every pipe underneath that thing was cracked and broken!

It was 15 minutes to the nearest store and we must have made 20 trips back and forth that first 24 hours, getting parts and tools, to make it livable. Luckily, we were not charged any rent for the first 6 months while we were fixing everything. It was a good trade, since we were in an adventurous mood!

Remember how I said that we were moving south to get away from the cold and snow? Well, the snow was coming down so hard in our new desert home that it was coming down sideward! That first night, trying to move all of our things in while it was snowing so hard, was discouraging and our girls were cold and tired. Karen, having been previously happy to get away from the snow-driven North was now questioning this move. Between the snow and the tall weeds, she wasn't sure this was such a great idea. Then, we met our "older than dirt", toothless new neighbor, Dan. He smiled and asked, "Are you guys Mormons? How'd you like to meet my sister? Ha ha ha ha!" We ended up accepting this as a fun part of a brand new adventure!

There were a few other neighbors that came over, as well. A few cute, older couples that lived on the row behind us just across the street. They all seemed very sweet and friendly. One of the couples offered to take the girls to their home and keep them warm and feed them cookies and hot chocolate while we got moved in enough to be able to put them to bed. We felt good about that and the girls were more than excited! They made fast friends with all of these new "grampas and grammas" and visited them every day for the next year and a half while we were living our new home.

The mobile home was so ugly that Karen tried to hide the fact it was ours by pretending our girls were being babysat by the poor family that lived there... She worked at a local health resort as a hiking guide at the base of Snow Canyon State Park and one day while hiking with the guests, they happened to walk past our humble little trailer. Our little daughters were out in the yard playing. They were so excited to see their mother, they ran to the weedy fence, jumping and giggling and waving at their mom! There was my sweet wife, hiking with doctors, lawyers, and all kinds of professional, wealthy people staying at the resort to get fit and healthy, and she was too embarrassed to let them think that poor humble mobile home was hers! She found herself telling these people that her girls were at the babysitters while she worked!

Though it was an embarrassment at times, we stayed there for a year and a half and were able to purchase that place dirt cheap. We then resold it for a down payment on an actual house. It was the beginning of a great new adventure!

Chapter 13

Linemen Versus Meter Men

Now, everybody knows the Linemen are the hard guys. They're the tough guys. They climb the poles. They touch the live lines with their hands. Even though they've got gloves on, they handle live power. They work in their bucket trucks and they dig holes in the ground. Well, the meter department is where the power company stuck me. We just ride scooters and jump fences and fight dogs. It's more of a girly job, rather than a guy job, so the linemen were always kind of making fun of me and teasing.

One day, one of the linemen slammed a Blow Snake up against my chest without me seeing it. Remember, I don't like snakes! Everybody got a laugh. *Ha ha ha!* My problem with that… Did I say I don't like snakes? I mean I hate snakes! I know I've got a phobia because just seeing them move gives me the heebie-jeebies. I just believe that if there's one rattler left heading towards extinction, kill it! Do me a favor, do the world a favor, and get rid of them. But that's my opinion and men have fought wars for me to have that freedom to voice it. I HATE snakes!

So, how do I get even? You know what? There's no such thing as getting even. Get ahead! And, so I did! I got me real good! Have you ever tried to get someone and you get yourself at the same time? Big backfire!! *This was way back in the days before people really started using pipe bombs.* I made a fake one that looked so real that it definitely made everyone in the warehouse have a quick thought to pray or panic! When they discovered it, it was under a newspaper in a pizza box!

Eventually, it ended up in a Christmas box with a note from the grateful people of the Arizona Strip to the management of their rural co-op for making the prices go up. It had a note that said it should be opened at the company Christmas party by the company PR man. The secretary was asked (by me) to not let it out of her possession until the party. She had asked me to help get the PR guy back for all the silly tricks that he would play on the secretaries every week, so this definitely would do the trick. The only problem was that she let it get away and then I heard on the radio for Car 15 to get to the office right away.

Oh man, did I get myself this time! I got myself so good that there were four unmarked cars, three City of St. George police cars, and a couple of county sheriff trucks all waiting for Car 15 to show up and defuse the bomb! The CEO was actually on the phone, sitting at the desk, taking care of business with his cowboy hat on and feet up! No fear in this dude at all! But the guy that opened the package was nowhere to be seen. I think a change of clothing might have been necessary!

I've been told that the city still has that on display for things *not* to do! And, as luck would have it, for the rest of that week the news was pelted with idiots blowing up mailboxes with pipe bombs and they weren't just any mailboxes, they were (of course) judge's mailboxes! That was the first we'd seen of pipe bombs on the news. What timing I had! That night the company Christmas party went on as scheduled and I attended with my poor wife (who did NOT want to go, due to the circumstances).

One other problem with this job was that dogs and I do not mix well. Remember my childhood story where I was bitten by 9 dogs before I was even eight years old? Well, now

I'm jumping fences to read meters, and I'm on their turf and they do not want me there. I was given a can of pepper spray and my boss had the nerve to tell me, "If you get bitten by one more dog, you're fired!" I was bitten by *two* dogs before I ended my career as a meter reader. Ironically though, it wasn't the dog bites that ended this job for me, but the fake bomb scare!

I soon found myself looking for new adventures. All because I really knew how to outdo myself quite well. Lesson learned! Sometimes you don't have to get ahead... or even. It's ok if someone else wins sometimes. Someone once asked me, "Do you want to be right, or do you want to be happy?" Maybe there was wisdom in that statement, after all. Think about that the next time you want to argue who's right with your spouse, significant other, business partner etc.

Have you ever known a born loser? Someone who just can't hold a job, always broke, bumming money, always has a story.... Well, this guy got all excited when he got an invitation to his 20th high school reunion. The invitation came from a corporate CEO that was his best friend in high school. He could hardly wait to see him and find out how he became so successful. He knew, because of their past friendship, this friend would be his mentor and teach him what he knew.

The reunion day arrived and they were visiting around a large table full of people. The loser asked the CEO what the secret of his success was.

The wealthy man said, "Ok, I'll tell you. It has to do with the good book. I would open the Bible and I would prayerfully drop my finger in a spot on the page that the book happened to open to. Whatever the word under my finger said is what I would do. The first time, the word was cattle, so I invested in cattle and they did me well. Then the second time, the word was oil, so I took the money from the cattle and invested in an Oil Company and we struck it rich! The third time, the word under my finger was flight, so I bought a little puddle jumper airline. It made it big and turned into Delta Airlines."

The loser was very grateful for this newfound wisdom and couldn't wait to get home to try it! With fervent prayer that night, he opened his Bible and faithfully dropped his finger down on the page. When he opened his eyes, he read the words "Chapter 13"!

Chapter 14

National Institute of Fitness, Snow Canyon State Park

The Segway music in my life, at this time, could've been a catchy little song from the band *Chumbawamba* titled "I get knocked down, but I get up again."

At the same time, I was working as a meter reader, before the fake bomb scare, I also had a second job at the National Institute of Fitness. This would become my primary place of work now. I worked there in the evenings and Saturdays. This was a fascinating place to me. They had those domed buildings that look like the sci-fi series on TV where bubbles would come down from out of space and pick people up who were trying to escape their prison. Nobody could ever escape. They would always show up when you least expected it and scoop you up inside of that bubble and fly you back to captivity. I just had to get a job there! But there were no jobs to be had except a massage therapy position.

When we first arrived in Southern Utah, the closest place I could find a job was the Peppermill Resort and Casino in Mesquite, Nevada, where I could put my trade from my previous life of being a bartender to work. Some of the locals noticed that I didn't smoke or drink and asked me if I was a Mormon.

I said, "Yes, I am."

Their reply? "Then why would you work in such a place as this?"

My answer was, "The Savior was rebuked by Peter for going into the den of iniquity. The Savior said, 'The sick are in need of a physician.' You people are pretty sick and I'm practicing medicine without a license!"

My coworker just laughed!

The tips were horrible, and I was not making enough money there. So along with the job change to become a meter reader, I asked Karen, "If I were to get a job as a massage therapist at the National Institute of Fitness, what would you think of that?"

She said, "You don't know the first thing about massage therapy. How are you going to get a job doing that?"

I said, "No, you didn't understand my question. I know that I can get the job as a massage therapist, if you're okay with me being in a room with a woman and the only thing between her naked body and me is a thin sheet and a bottle of oil! Now my question again, how do you feel about me being in a room with naked women? Are you okay with this?"

She said, "You're crazy! I'm okay with you and I'm okay with our relationship, but I still think you're crazy if you think you can get a job out there when you've never even had a massage and you don't know the first thing about it. You're crazy!"

Well, my thought was, "How difficult can it be? If I just have someone give me a massage and I take notes on what they did and then repeat it... it should be no big deal!"

My biggest concern in doing a treatment on someone was how to keep it modest and how to keep the sheets and towels tight. I wanted it to be comfortable and professional for both my client and myself. So, I bought a treatment for myself to learn how to tuck the sheets tight to keep it modest. I then practiced on my wife and family. And... I got the job! For the next several years, I received the highest acclaims for my talent and it made me want to learn more to be even better. In

Utah, at that time, a massage therapist didn't need a license if they worked at an educational or fitness facility.

I started each of my treatments off with a prayer in my mind. Of course, you can't talk out loud when you're giving someone a treatment. If I started praying out loud, they would run out of the room and I would get fired! So, they all thought that I was fluffing their aura or zoning in or gaining my Chi when I was praying quietly to myself. Whatever they were thinking was really none of my concern. My concern was asking Heavenly Father to help this person, whom I was about to work on, to enjoy their session and feel comfortable enough to ask questions about why I was living in Utah, what brought me here from New England, what got me into massage therapy, etc. I wanted to have a meaningful conversation that might change them for the better in some way, as well as feeling physically rejuvenated for exercise the next day.

On one of my bus charters I drove to California, years earlier, there was a chaperone who worked in the twin towers in New York City. He told me of a healing laser he was working with called a Bioptron, from Switzerland. I could not stop thinking about that healing light, especially now that I was working with people with pain. I got in touch with him and he put me in touch with the inventors. I purchased a few and started working with them. The company actually put me, along with Karen's mom and dad, on their video of testimonials to tell how good the Bioptron works.

Because it was from Switzerland and needed to have FDA approval for pain relieving abilities, the Bioptron would need to go through years of testing that would cost millions of dollars and the company was not interested in doing that. They closed the account for pain relief and it was only used as a skin enhancer in the United States. However, people were not interested in paying $350 for something that just improved their skin. So, I took it to a convention trying to make some sales. I was hoping to come home a winner and show Karen that she married an excellent provider! I came home with a big "L" on my forehead, as in "Loser", with no sales and down $500 for the booth rental. I also owed the company for all the lasers.

At the convention, there was a company from Brisbane, Australia, that had technicians fixing everybody's pain with their fingers! By just flicking the body with light touch here, light touch there, the pain was gone. All these people would've possibly bought a lamp, but they were all pain-free because of this light touch therapy they were getting right before coming to my booth. *Even though it was not approved by the FDA for pain relief, it still did get rid of pain.*

I was so irritated at that light touch group that I went down in frustration and asked the silver haired guy, "What about when your fingers are in Australia and these people have a little baby that's teething and can't go to sleep because of pain at two in the morning? Where are your fingers then to get rid of their pain? None of these people are interested in my lamp because you're fixing everybody, but you can't fix them when you're not around!"

I then suggested he take my lamps and we would split the profit for any that sold, but he responded, "No, no, we're not into doing anything but this."

His therapy was called *Bowen,* after a physicist in Australia who created the technique. Although, there are stories that say that the Aborigines were taught the technique by some visiting Catholic nuns. All I knew for sure was that Bowen cost me money and I did not like any of them. As fate would have it, about two weeks after that trade show, a friend of mine named Merlene called me and said, "What do you think about Bowen, that light touch therapy?"

I said, "I hate them!"

"Well, we love them because we all felt better with one

treatment," she responded. "But now we need to follow up two weeks later and there is no one around here who does it. So, we were hoping you'd go learn it and come back to work on us."

"No, I'm not interested in them at all," I told her. "They cost me too much money, so I don't have any money to go take their training. Besides, they're all the way down under in Australia."

Merlene never did take *no* for an answer. She had it all figured out. She and her friends would put their credit cards together to buy me a ticket and pay for the course. When I came back, I would work on them in trade to pay it off. Despite my prejudice, I knew Bowen was a good therapy, because of the fact that nobody had pain when they came to my booth after being at their booth. Now I had to go ask my wife what she thought of me taking a few weeks off to go learn this therapy that had cost us money by ruining our booth sales with the Bioptron.

Once again, she thought I was a little crazy. They had already cost me money and now I wanted to take more money and throw it into the wind. Our house payment was due, but she said, "If you feel inspired to do it, go ahead. I'll support you, but I still think you're crazy!" I think when I hear the word "crazy" it just delights me. It thrills me that I can do things that no one else wants to do or can do. I love a challenge and, when my wife says an idea is crazy, something inside me hits the dopamine button in my brain cells and fills me with such a thrill to prove myself. I can do this! I'm a winner!

There happened to be a class in Connecticut. So, off I flew, back East. I rented a car and drove to Watertown, Connecticut. I took the class and then drove back to New England (Boston) to do a quick treatment on my dad's knee before I checked in at the airport to fly home. He was scheduled for surgery a few weeks later and I decided it would be cool to try this new therapy on him. He had instant pain relief and no more limping! The next day he called me and said, "Paul, no smoke...the pain is still gone, but the swelling is gone now too! What am I going to do about my surgery? I've been months planning this with the best surgeon there is here in Boston. Now I don't know what to do. Do I keep my appointment with this guy? He's the best and it takes forever to get into his office for an appointment, let alone surgery!"

My advice to my dad was, "If it ain't broke, don't fix it!"

His reply was, "That's easy for you to say. How long is this fix going to last?"

"Dad, I have no idea! I just know that this thing cost me a fortune in lost sales and I am in debt up to my eyeballs now with credit card debt! But, in the class I just left, over 30 people are now certified. More than half of those therapists had problems that were resolved in that class and they teach that it's a two to five-year fix. So, give it two to five years and see what happens."

Dad never got the knee surgery. He never needed it! And I paid off all my credit card debt under 30 days and I made my house payment on time! Around this same time, my friend Merlene called me and told me to come to her place right away. She said there were some oils she wanted me to see. Oils made from flowers. They're called essential oils, not crude oil. There was a brand-new company called Young Living Essential Oils. The founder was a descendent of Brigham Young, the second President of the LDS church.

Years earlier, he had been in a lumber camp accident and badly injured his spine, confining him to a wheelchair. The essential oils helped him to get out of his wheelchair and he was able to run in the Boston Marathon! When Merlene said Boston, I was on that just as lickety-split as I could. Slight problem. Karen and I had promised each other (in fact, I'm pretty sure we pinky swore) we would never join another Multi Level Marketing company, because back when I was working in the coal mines, we tried to retire early from the coal mines with "Amway". We had built to the direct level twice and both groups had quit and we had no more friends! *People tend to shy away from people that are in a new MLM and are over excited to share it with everyone and anyone that breaths!*

But Merlene doesn't take no for an answer! She was a single parent mom and had been taking care of her kids as a waitress. She had given up waitressing and picked up that 150-pound phone. *That's what it felt like at times.* She kept calling people until they would listen and join. And join they did, over and over, again, and again, and again. She had done that with another company and she was determined to do it again with Young Living Essential Oils. This company seemed to have the best of all the products on the market. *It seems that a lot of those MLM's were like burning tumbleweeds. They come and go as quick as that.*

Well, I spent the next two years traveling with Merlene. We held oil classes for people, demonstrating the oils on people and teaching them about all the amazing products the company had to offer. I drove her motorhome from North to South (mostly the West Coast) and we had a good routine down. On my mission, President Hart had taught us "Thee lift me and me lift thee and we'll both ascend together." Merlene adopted that and we enjoyed every moment of those journeys from city to city and state to state for two years.

On one trip, the traffic got backed up quite bad on I-15. Just before it came to a stop, on the inside passing lane, some guy three cars behind us was not paying attention and slammed into the car in front of him, which caused a four-car pile-up! I saw him in my rearview mirror and pulled off to the inside lane and *Bam!* He hit a van, which then hit 3 more stopped cars in a row! *Bam! Bam! Bam!* The driver of the van wanted out to beat the dummy that had just caused him severe pain! Pinned against the dash and steering wheel and the driver's seat. He was screaming for that driver to "get over here!"

I quickly put Joy (rose) oil on my right hand and went over to shake his hand, all the while telling him I saw the whole thing and that I was on his side. The spirit of Gandhi overcame him. He calmed down and never mentioned that guy again. Over 20 minutes later, he was rushed off to the ER. I saw Joy oil change the evil Mr. Hyde back into the kind Dr. Jekyll that day! After that day, the commission checks started to come in from Young Living and they started getting bigger and bigger. So, we got excited and started doing more classes. Merlene was now pulling in over $10K a month! I was doing about $2k!

The resort I did massage therapy at did not like multilevel marketing and they did not take any guest complaints lightly. It was very difficult for me to not talk to people about this part of my life, when they would ask questions about me or my family. It's just in me to want to share with others the things that are important to me and the things that make me happy. Like I said before, at the beginning of each massage session, I'd always say my silent prayer. Then my first question after my little prayer would be, "I have a story called "The Plane Maker", by Marvin Payne, who just happened to give me permission to perform it... Or the next 50 minutes can be just quiet and peaceful. Your choice, what will it be?"

I knew the ones who chose the story would gain the most from the treatment and draw closer to Heavenly Father through the Holy Ghost during our visits. And I know I was being challenged by the adversary to not talk about the "Plane Maker" or my personal life's story. At one point, I had been told, "One more complaint and you will be terminated!" It was like a game of Russian Roulette. I never knew when I would cross the boundaries of spiritual personal space and they would write a note in their comment card or just put a few words on a pre-printed comment card and I would be fired! As I needed the money and it was $35 per hour plus tips, I did not want to lose this job. With faith, and beginning each treatment with a prayer, I decided I had no worries at all. I knew my Heavenly Father would fight my battles for me doing his work. I had many choice experiences with many guests at this great resort, which is now called Red Mountain Resort.

One day, a beautiful lady from New York scheduled an appointment with me after a hard week's worth of exercise and mountain climbing. The session started out as it normally does, with a quick silent prayer. Right off the bat, we started a conversation and she asked the question, "What brings you all the way out to the Utah desert from Boston?" I was delighted with her inquiring mind, knowing where this was going to take us for the next 50 minutes. But something disturbing happened halfway through the treatment...and the conversation. My client was face down, with her head in the face rest of the massage table. This is usually an extremely comfortable position, but she was troubled. Raising up on her elbows to wipe the tears from her eyes, she said, "Stop please, just stop!"

I happened to be testifying of Christ's visit to the pre-Columbian Indians, and my journey to becoming a very active Mormon. Her mascara running down her face gave me a chill. "This is it!" I thought. "I'm going to lose my job!" But then she started to tell me her story. She said that she married into a very high-ranking mafia family in New York and her free agency to do certain things was very limited, to say the least. She had been mourning the loss of her grandmother that she loved so ardently and had come to the resort to help her in her grieving. She was also trying to get away from the nightmares that she was having over her grandmother's death!

As a child, her grandmother would sit her on her knee and teach her things by telling her stories. Lots of stories. She had felt so close to her grandma that every day she would hurry home from school to hear more of the stories! And, as an adult, spending time with her grandmother and feeling her embrace and enjoying her beautiful smile had helped her through many rough times. She was so full of love! With the rest of her family life being involved around the mafia, she could not get enough of her grandma to balance her life out! With her grandmother's death, she was devastated! Now those cherished moments were no more. Her anguish in mourning that loss found her deeply depressed, praying to God for help.

The help came in the form of a dream that she started having. A dream of her grandma telling her stories as a child. This thrilled her! She enjoyed these re-occurring dreams and they became more and more detailed. In fact, this became a problem in her relationship with her husband, because she would always want to retire to bed early so that she could dream about her grandma. This upset her husband. Then, something terrible happened to her dreams. They turned into nightmares! Her grandmother would be telling her the stories, but in the middle of telling her the stories her grandmother's face was blocked by a pair of strange looking shoes and she could no longer see her grandmother's beautiful smile.

This was the reason she had come to the resort. She thought maybe some exercise and healthy eating would help put balance back into her life and somehow get her away from the nightmares. She did not want to see those shoes blocking her grandmothers' face. No longer were the dreams desirable or even sleep, for fear that they would come back as they always did! She didn't understand what it meant and why it kept happening. The shoes interrupted the beautiful stories from her grandmother. Stories that she knew were true. So, with mascara running down her tear-stained face, she pointed to my feet and said, "Those are the shoes in my nightmares!"

Ok, now I knew I was fired! That was until she explained about the feeling around her. The feeling that was present during my story of becoming a Mormon and of my journey to Utah was the same feeling that she would always have when her grandmother was telling her similar stories as a child. Her grandmother had told her how she had joined the Mormon Church. She'd taught her how angels had visited Joseph Smith. How he was given an ancient record on plates of gold and told to interpret them. They became The Book of Mormon. She was told how Joseph prayed and had his prayer answered in a sacred Grove in New York, not far from where she lived. God introduced his son Jesus Christ and actually spoke to Joseph.

"As you were telling me your story," she said. "This feeling came over me... that same feeling I had with my grandma. I opened my eyes and saw the shoes that you're wearing are the very same shoes that covered my grandma's face in all those dreams. I finally understand the dreams and that she was giving me a message through you!"

Well, I didn't lose my job that day and I still have those shoes in my closet. I will never throw those shoes away. I don't know the rest of her life story. I don't know what this beautiful woman went home to do with this answer that she received that day. I would love it if I could be like Paul Harvey and tell you the rest of the story. Maybe in the Celestial world to come we can hear it from her own words. If you ponder this story as I have, you will realize that a number of things needed to take place before this "ordinary miracle" could have occurred.

First, this woman needed to have a loving grandmother full of cool stories.

Second, she had to have the dreams and the nightmares.

Third, she had to pick the right resort out of hundreds worldwide, book the time to stay, buy a flight and get to the resort.

Fourth, I needed to get a job working at that resort.

Fifth, I needed to be working the night she had her appointment.

Sixth, my wife bought me a pair of turquoise dress slacks. *The same look Don Johnson wore on the TV show* Miami Vic*e, which was really popular back then.* I was with her and bought the very unique matching color double-laced white and turquoise tennis shoes. They are one of a kind! They had to be manufactured of the same exact design that was in her nightmare. They had to be placed in the store for me to see, with the color tying into the slacks Karen bought for my birthday.

And lastly, I had to wear them on the evening of her treatment… Yeah, just another ordinary miracle…

I'm no different than anybody else. I look forward to vacation time. I look forward to going to the lake or to see a new movie. I look forward to going on a date with my wife to that new restaurant in town. Normal week days pass by and we look forward to the weekend because that's when something cool is planned… All the rest get chocked up as days that really don't count for much. But that night I was just working. Another appointment, another hour out of my evening. Another nice person that I get to chat with for a moment in time and then they go home back to New York or California or Spain or wherever they live. Unless they come back next year, I'll probably never see them again.

The creator of this wonderful planet designed each one of us with a special need to fulfill while walking on this earth. Until we figure out who we are, where we came from and where we're going when this life is over, the mysteries just keep piling up, often unnoticed. If you are not prayerfully asking for miracles and looking for ways to serve your fellow men every single day, even you will not notice these ordinary miracles piling up in front of you.

"We live but once, the years of my childhood, when once past, are past forever. It matters not how ardently we wish to live them over, it avails us nothing. So, it is with the other stages of life. The past is no longer ours. It is gone beyond our reach. What we have made it, it shall remain. There is no power in Heaven or on earth that can change it. The record of our Past stands fourth in bold ineffaceable characters, open to the all-seeing eye of God. There it stands, and one day we shall give an account of it. The present moment alone is ours. Now is thy treasure possessed unawares. Today is a day, which we never had before, which we shall never have again. It rose from the great ocean of eternity, and again sinks into its unfathomable depths."

— *James E. Talmage,* Leaves of Gold

Paul Joseph Brennan

Chapter 15

Which Home Should We Buy

I worked in the meter department at DEREA (Dixie Escalante Rural Electrical Association) for a couple of years, until our area was split and another friend took care of Littlefield Arizona, while I took care of what's called Bloomington Hills. On occasion, I would take his truck and repair water heaters down in his area and spend the day servicing customers. My timing did not work out as good as I had planned one day. It was almost quitting time and I had a half hour ride to get home to give the truck back to my work associate, my best friend. So, I drove faster than I should have up the canyon called the Virgin River Gorge. The highway patrol man said I was clocked at about 95 mph. I know I was doing that plus, but what is more important is the conversation I was having in the cab of the truck while driving against the clock. *I was chatting with God.*

Karen and I were trying to decide on two homes that were in our budget to purchase. One was in an area that the bishop was a highway patrolman and the other was in an area where the bishop worked for the telephone company as a repairman. Now, I liked the house better that was located in the highway patrolman's ward, but CDL truck drivers and highway patrolmen are like the old cowboys and Indians. Not a good mix!

Side note… In the Mormon church there's no paid clergy,

so there's no worry about getting fired from your calling if you give a lousy talk. In fact, everything in the church is done for free and on donated time. All the classes are taught, all the toilets are cleaned, etc., by the bishop calling individuals to accept the jobs and we all do our part.

Now, I just knew that if this highway patrolman bishop would ask me to do something, I'd tell him to pound sand. "Because, you know Heavenly Father, all Highway Patrolmen are the same...you're guilty until proven innocent, especially if you're trying to cross the border of another state and your logbooks are not up to square, or your permits aren't in order or one of them might be a week outdated or you might've purchased 30 gallons too much fuel and you're overweight on one axle... No matter what it is, it's a $100 fine and it takes an hour or two out of your day! I can't move into the ward where the bishop is a highway patrolman. You and I both know they are no good!"

So, I'm being pulled over at this exact time in my communication with God. Ironic, right?!... I know! This Arizona patrolman adjusts his belt and leans into the window and asks, "You didn't even see where I clocked you at, did you? Good hiding spot huh?!"

"Officer, I am very late! It's after quitting time and the guys at work are waiting on this truck to get back to the warehouse so they can go home!"

"Do you know how fast you were traveling up that canyon?" he asked.

"Yes, I do, because I'm late. Just give me the ticket, because I've got to get this truck back to the warehouse..."

He interrupted me and said, "You know what? You just need to slow this thing down a little. I had you clocked at over 95 mph. Just touch the ground once in a while and stay in between the white lines! Now go get this back to the warehouse safely and have a nice day."

I looked at him with shock in my eyes and asked, "Do you mean I'm not getting a ticket? Thank you! Thank you, Officer!"

As I drove off, I looked up into the heavens and laughed out loud at how much of an idiot I must've sounded like with my testosterone driven, CDL truck driven, chauvinistic pig-headed view of highway patrolmen. Smokey the bear and Holy the ghost! Was I ever wrong! I bought the house in the ward boundary where the bishop was the highway patrolman and he and I have been the best of friends for over 27 years now! In fact, you may have even enjoyed his sugar-free gourmet chocolate named after his daughter Amber Lyn. That's right! Amber Lyn Chocolates sold at Costco and various other locations. When they give out free samples, it's hard to turn down and then it's hard to not buy a box!

Sometimes we just need to be open to new ideas and stop being so stubborn that we think we know everything. I would have missed out on a great friend, a great bishop and the realization that we should not judge people by their stereotypes. Lesson learned!

There was a preacher that was very nervous about moving into a new area and giving his first sermon. He worked on it for at least six weeks to be sure he was ready. He'd gotten his family all moved in and situated, and he knew if he didn't do a good job they could fire him. So, under all this pressure he was ready to deliver the most incredible, inspired sermon you could imagine coming from a mere human. When the time came, there was only one cowboy from this fairly large town that showed up. So, the preacher walked down into the middle of the almost empty Chapel and informed the cowboy of his dilemma. He's ready to deliver the most promising sermon, but with only one parishioner, what should he do?

The cowboy tipped his hat up and gave that preacher a bit of his wisdom. He said, "Now, if I had only one cow show up expecting to eat, I'd feed it."

The preacher relaxed and thanked the cowboy and went back up to the podium and gave what he felt was the most amazing sermon ever. But then he saw that the cowboy was asleep and actually snoring pretty loudly. So, he went down and nudged the cowboy.

When he woke up, the preacher said, "I was doing what you said. I was delivering my speech because you're here and I'm feeding you like you suggested. But you were asleep, so I'm kind of at a loss that you fell asleep on me."

The cowboy said, "Preacher, I said if one cow showed up I would feed it, but I didn't say I'd feed it the whole load!"

Chapter 16

Baby Joey

While we were still living in the little ugly mobile home, 7½-year-old Tiffany came in to us one morning and asked us if we were going to ever have another baby. We told her we weren't sure, since we were very nervous after what happened with the twins. She proceeded to inform us that we had to because her baby sister had talked to her in her dreams and told her that she wanted to come down now and that we wouldn't listen. Tiffany was adamant that we let her sister come be part of our family now. We figured Tiff just really wanted a little sister so bad that she made up the story. Well, the next morning she was crying when she said that her little sister talked to her again and was really serious that she was ready to be part of our family. This got us thinking and we decided it might be time to try again.

Karen got pregnant immediately! She was hiking every day with the resort, she was in great health and we were feeling good that this pregnancy would go well. The doctors had told us that she should be fine and there were no negative effects from the last pregnancy. Of course, we knew that this was another girl, since up to that point, that's all we knew… and, of course, this had to be the little sister that had communicated with Tiffany those two nights in a row that got us to even consider having another baby. When the ultrasound tech asked Karen if she wanted to know the gender, Karen let him know that she didn't need him to tell her that it was a girl. There was no question in her mind!

Well, the ultrasound tech begged to differ! He saw something that didn't look like girl parts! How could this be? We were all in total shock! What would we do with a boy? And where was our baby girl that had spoken to Tiff? Hmmm…well, after the shock wore off, we were pretty excited!

Karen was still working as a hiking guide at the resort when she was almost 8 months along. Of course, at this point, she did some of the easier hikes. One day, she was hiking up the road with a group of guests and they were just talking about everyday stuff when Karen mentioned that her washer broke that morning. Well, one of the guests overheard the conversation and thought she said her water broke. You can imagine how concerned she was thinking that here Karen is on a hike when her water had broken that morning. The misunderstanding was cleared up quickly and they all had a good laugh!

On another day, I decided to hike with them and not many of the guests had realized that we were married to each other. I was being a little flirty with Karen and a few guests got concerned thinking, "Here's this company massage therapist flirting with this girl. Doesn't he see that she's pregnant?" When they finally realized we were actually husband and wife they were quite relieved. We had another good laugh!

The pregnancy went perfect and, right as we were able to move into our new home, Joseph Paul Brennan was born. Needless to say, he got lots of attention! The girls were 7 and 9 by this time. Jessica, having been the baby for 7 years was a little jealous and had a hard time with this new little baby taking her mama's attention away from her. But it didn't take long for her to also fall in love with Joey and the whole family spoiled the heck out of the kid from then on out. New home.

New baby. Life was good!

Joey grew into a busy, curious toddler and kept us all chasing him around and making sure he was happy, spoiled and safe. Like any two-year-old, Joey loved to discover new places and loved climbing. Going up or down stairs is magic to little people. On one occasion, he was in the kitchen and started heading toward the doorway. This led to the steps that went down to my office, which had a concrete floor with a linoleum cover. As he was nearing the steps, he tripped! In seconds, he was falling face first down the 3 steps onto the floor below.

Now, this wouldn't have been life threatening, but while he was falling, he bumped an empty quart mason jar that was sitting at the top of the steps off the step and it fell along with Joey. As it fell, it broke and landed right side up with a large 3-inch spike (like a stiletto) of glass sticking straight up. Joey landed right at the same time and somehow caught himself with his arms in a push up position just before the spike would have gone through his skin and through his heart! All of this happened as his mom stood watching in horror! It all happened so fast that she couldn't get to him quick enough. The spike of the jar, though it didn't puncture the skin, left a tiny mark on his skin… a reminder of how fragile life can be and God's mercy. Karen ran to Joey and grabbed him to her chest. She held him tightly, shaking and crying and grateful for the fact that he was safe and still alive!

Every parent holds great aspirations for their children to become better than they themselves aspire. When the doctors wanted to do a surgery preventing this young man from being born and when this glass stiletto spike was only a hair's breadth away from taking this boy's life but didn't, I know that God has a special calling for this boy to do. When he was very young, we were sitting in the back of our church and Joey asked his mom and I, "Why do some people have a ring of light around them?" He was so innocent and figured we could all see what he saw. When he was all grown up and was working on an oil rig in Wyoming for a short time, one of the company men, who was known for using foul language and prided himself on getting rid of newbies by bullying them, said "What is it about you that makes me feel awkward about swearing in front of you? Nobody in the oil field has ever made me feel this way! This only happens at home when I'm around my wife and kids!"

Joey has that effect on a lot of people. He never speaks guile. He has never spoken a foul word. As we have watched him navigate through an 8+ year marriage that ended in divorce, he still chooses to speak no negative! As each trial teaches us life lessons, he is a better person today because of these experiences and the way he has chosen to get through them. Heavenly Father blesses us as we choose to honor him by being the kind of person he knows we can be, especially during trials. Then after the trial comes the blessing. Joey has been blessed immensely! He is now planning a wedding with the love of his life, Avery, and we are so happy to share in their joy! True eternal joy. We must have done something right in the parenting department or we are just very blessed, because we have amazing, awesome kids and grandkids! There is definitely joy in our journey of life and parenthood. Whatever trials we've been through and whatever trials we have yet to go through, they are worth it because we get to keep our family through eternity!

There were two brothers in their early 30's that still lived at home with their mom and one had a cat that he dearly loved. He went a little overboard taking care of and spoiling his cat. He hand-fed it with a silver spoon, bought diamond studded collars for it, etc... One day, he had to leave for a business trip so he begged his brother to please take good care of his feline friend the way he did. His brother agreed, figuring, how hard can it be to take care of a dumb cat. Well, as the cat lover was away, he called his brother every day to check on his beloved cat.

One particular day he called, he asked his brother, "How is my lovely cat?"

"Your cat is dead," replied the uncaring brother.

"What?! How can you tell me my cat is dead?! That's my baby! I love that cat! Don't just tell me my cat's dead!"

To which the uncaring brother replied, "What do you want me to say? The cat is dead!"

"Well at least you could break it to me easy! Make up a story. Like, maybe the first day tell me he was on the roof, and maybe the next day tell me he fell off and you had to take him to the vet, and maybe then the next day say that they did everything they could, but he didn't make it through the night! Don't just tell me my cat's dead! Dang! By the way, how's mom?"

"She's on the roof....?"

Paul Joseph Brennan

Chapter 17

Buried Alive

It was a beautiful sunlit morning. Two friends started out enjoying the day with small talk about stuff that really doesn't matter. Though we were construction dudes, we both tried to never use foul language. *Which is very different than most construction sites.* I was Jody's home teacher. Jody was a rough-cut strong guy that could rival any biker, but he had a great heart. If the kind of dog a person has tells what kind of guy you are…Jody raised Akitas. If you've never seen an Akita, look them up and you'll see what I mean.

Being Jody's home teacher, the responsibility of checking on his family's well-being was up to me. It's a little like the welcome wagon giving the new move-in the information on local jobs, venders, good doctors, etc. Jody was grateful for my home visits and the gospel messages that I would bring to his family once a month. This is what a Mormon Church home teacher does. He makes sure the family's needs are all covered…Food, rent, etc.… temporary support until things get better, as well as spiritual messages.

Like I said at the beginning of the book, the guy that owned the house we were working at forgot to shut the sprinklers off, so the trench was very wet and soggy and unstable. Water had filled the trench the night before and I used the bucket of the backhoe to scoop some of the water out.

We'd actually had to wait a day for the water to seep the rest of the way out. So, there we were, worried about whether or not the flood had changed the flow or the slope of the pipe. We just wanted to check it and get back out of that trench before anything happened. But as we were leveling the pipe, the unthinkable did happen! The whole side of the trench gave way and came down on me!

Jody saw it happening and got out quickly enough that he was only buried up to his knees. He actually said, "Wow, that was close!" Then, he turned to look back at me and realized I had not been so lucky. He freaked out! He got himself free of the mud and assessed the situation. It was then he realized that both of our shovels were buried somewhere down in the trench with me. He remembered that, for some reason, he had thrown a third shovel on the truck that morning. Was this part of my miracle that day? YES! There is no doubt about it! There was no other reason for him throwing that third shovel on the truck except that God knew he would need it.

Jody ran to grab the shovel and yelled for the neighbor to call 911. *The house we were working on had no phone connection because the cave in ripped the phone line off the house and severed it.* I would have to say that if you ever get buried you'd want Jody to be there to do the digging to get you out! He was a wild man and had the muscle and stamina to back it up! Especially after his adrenalin kicked in. He told my wife later that all he could think of was having to tell her what had happened. He was determined to make this story end good and not bad.

When I first realized what was happening, after the initial shock of being caught off guard, I was pretty angry with God for letting this happen to me. I felt that I was a pretty good guy and didn't deserve this. I decided that God had to be insane to let this happen to me! I remember thinking how I had always tried to do all my home teaching; I was a good husband and father; I tried to treat my fellow man the way I would want to be treated... I really didn't deserve this! Take the guy down the street that's a jerk! Not me! But I have always known that, with enough faith, I could get out of whatever situation I would find myself in. So, I figured that with the position I ended up in with one arm up above my head, and a shovel up against my chest, I was almost in a correct position for my right arm to be held up to the square.

With all the faith I had, I commanded the dirt to be lifted off me. I tried to stand up, fully expecting to be out of the situation. Well, it didn't work. So, I did it again, with all the faith and emphasis that I could muster. The second time, it still didn't work! Each time I tried to stand up, it imploded more mud and more pressure to the point that it was totally unbearable, even more than before. At that point, I was angry and being crushed with panic. I could feel every footstep above me and each one felt like a thousand tons! I felt like I could actually feel the "Nike" logo on the bottom of their shoes. I was wishing they would get off of the dirt above me! I'm sure they had no idea what an impression they were making on me! They were just trying to save my life.

The dirt was continuous in its compaction, increasing the pain and inability to breathe. Each time I exhaled, it was impossible to breath air back in. With each second that passed, there was a degree of hope lost and despair took its place. At a certain point, the maddening panic and anger towards God and pain gave way to a different kind of prayer. One that emergences from the center of your soul, knowing that you're going to meet your creator. The words were most devout in humility, submitting to "his will be done" and not mine, and meaning it without any ire; resolute, unconditional submission. At this moment in time, I gained a peace in my soul with the voice of Admiral Hart, my old mission president, bringing total recall to his miraculous story of being buried alive under water at sea, with an entire ship crushing him into the ocean floor. I had heard this story at our first interview 20 years earlier and had somehow forgotten it until this prayer.

Here is the story written from President C. Monroe Hart's own journal:

"During WWII, a Navy Lieutenant Engineer and Qualified Deep Sea Diver found himself under the keel of the U.S. Merchant Ship which had been torpedoed and had been driven aground on the rocky Cape Hatteras Beach, North Carolina. He was wearing the Navy's (then) shallow water diving gear with an air and lifeline tended from a barge alongside the stranded torpedoed ship. Suddenly a huge Atlantic Ocean Breaking wave hit the coast line lifting the grounded ship up and then dropping it down very hard- crushing the Lieutenant diver between the keel and the rocky bottom.

"His airline from the barge alongside was also pinned down on the rocks sealing off his air supply. His left arm was pinned across his chest. His right arm was over his head and crushed down on the rocks. With the airline closed his diving mask collapsed down on his face as he tried to breathe. Pinned down, unable to move and without air, there came to him the sudden realization that his situation was hopeless. And with it came maddening panic.

"But the young Lieutenant had been taught and taught by his mother to pray to his Father in Heaven- who cared about him. In pain with his mask collapsed on his face and unable to breathe- it was a hasty prayer- but devout. Then suddenly there came upon him a feeling of quiet calm. His panic vanished and he could think. With that calm came the realization that there was a tiny pulse of air coming into his mask. Not enough, but---

"Then the Lieutenant knew that somehow he had to stay conscious so he could think. He began just barely to sniff to stay conscious. After several minutes he began to feel his right hand and found that he could move his thumb. With his thumb, he moved a small rock. That freed his

forefinger. Then another rock and another… He could tell that the Diver Tender on the Barge was trying to signal him by tugging his lifeline, which was pinned down under the ship 10 feet away. Soon, both arms and his body were sufficiently free for him to move. He sniffed and rested, then holding his breath he cut his lifeline and air line with his knife and inched his way to the side of the ship opposite of the barge. Swimming to the surface, he filled his lungs with air! He was overwhelmed with the thought of what a blessing AIR is! And he felt unspeakable gratitude for the blessings of his Father in Heaven.

"After regaining his strength, he swam around the stern of the ship to the barge, climbed aboard, without a word picked up a crowbar and moved aside the two sailors who were still pushing back and forth on that hand air pump, then threw it overboard into the sea. He returned to Washington, sat down at his desk and wrote an All Navy (ALNAV) message directing all Navy units to dispose of all diving hand-driven air pumps and immediately requisition the new shallow water gasoline driven air pump. He took the message to Admiral Broschek, the Director of Maintenance, U.S. Navy and slammed it down on his desk! Admiral Broschek read the ALNAV, looked at the stern face of his Lieutenant, nodded his head and signed the message. The next day after the huge wave had moved the tanker it was re-floated."

With the recollection of this story, it restored hope. It restored faith instantly. Not that I was going to live, but that it was okay either way. Even though I was still being crushed, and was still in pain, and still could not get a breath, the maddening panic was gone. I could hear my friend Jody yelling for me, and I felt empathy for his situation and how he must be feeling. If I died, I wanted to leave an impression on him of something funny. At that moment, I felt the mud cave off my backside, which exposed part of my butt that was parallel to my head because I was in a bent position. I knew that it was far too late at this point for him to get to my face so I could breathe. It would take too long! I remember thinking how I wished I could convey this thought to him, "Oh, that my ass had nostrils that I might breathe one last breath of foul air before I die…" so that at least when I didn't make it, he could always look upon it and have a chuckle. That's the last thing I remember on this side of the veil. *Remember what the veil is… it's the veil of forgetfulness. It works really well!* I don't remember much of anything I experienced from that point, but the ones I do remember are too sacred to share publicly.

My next full recollection was like coming out of a dream. I felt the "dog-digging" hyper hands of Jody, pulling the wet sand away from my face so that I could breathe. When I opened my eyes and smiled, the smile was coming from my understanding that I was going to live and not die. The first thing I remember seeing was half a dozen faces looking down at me smiling. Those were the faces of the EMTs and a few friends, as well as Jody. I'll never forget Jody's smile.

The EMTs were going through their routine emergency response regimen and I remember threatening one of them that if he strapped me down, I'd find him later and hurt him! I was restricted in my communication in my weakened state, so I had him come down by my face to whisper this to him. He was trying to straighten out my leg, which was bent up against my chest. I had been in a very twisted, bent, pressur- ized state for so long that any movement hurt, but especially trying to lay flat. I felt better in fetal position. He told the other guys they'd have to transport me without straightening my leg out.

They got me to the Emergency Room at the hospital and did an amazing number of tests on me for the next few hours. I was in severe pain, but glad to breathe and be alive. Karen hadn't shown up yet to the hospital and I had been told they couldn't find her. We didn't have cell phones back then, so there was no way to find her until she got home from wherever she was. Karen's mom drove to the accident site as soon as she got the phone call about what had happened, then followed the ambulance to the hospital. Karen's dad waited on the corner at the turnoff for his daughter to pass so he could tell her what had happened and get her to me.

After many tests on me for anything that would have been affected from such an accident, the doctors finally told me that I was a miracle! All the tests came back normal. They couldn't find any problems from the accident and, even though I was in horrible pain, they were sending me home. Luckily, Karen had arrived at the hospital and took me home. The pain I was in, they said, was because of the pressure I had been under for such a long time and the strange position I had been in. My muscles and bones had been pushed on so hard that my whole body was like a big bruise. My chest bone kept popping in and out. My organs were in distress from being pinched in the bent position I was crushed in. My whole body was in shock. But I told my kids, "Don't worry if you hear daddy scream during the night with pain. I am ok, and I am alive, and that's good! Don't let it scare you! Pain is a sign of life. Silence would have meant that I went to Heaven."

I was happy to be alive. I'd walk around and do things like smell the roses on the rosebushes. I didn't laugh much because life was sacred and serious, and I was in pain. My family was used to me being a clown and being silly and making them laugh all the time. It was a little weird for them, but they tried to understand why. I remember once getting frustrated at the girls for arguing over a shirt that one had borrowed from the other. It had a stain on it and Tiff was mad at Jess for ruining it. I told them, "Don't you understand that the shirt doesn't matter! Life is sacred!" Karen had to remind me that the accident didn't happen to them and they were just normal teenagers.

But my experience had a great impact on me and for a few months, it affected the whole family! Karen and the kids had to lower me and raise me in and out of bed. I couldn't do it on my own. Karen also helped me get dressed and tie my shoes, etc. There was a lot I couldn't do but they were happy to help. We were just happy to be a family and have more time together. I couldn't work, so finances were scarce. We had to refinance our house to live because the people that we had been doing the work for were angry at me for getting buried and did not want it to affect their homeowner's insurance by making a claim. I called them one Monday night and told them not to worry. I would rather take care of my own situation than cause unkind feelings. My personal integrity and honor are far more important than any dollar amount, even in my desperate situation.

Thank goodness that I had some equity in my house that I could take care of my family while I was recuperating. If you always try to do the right thing and keep your integrity intact, Heavenly Father will provide a way out of any situation. Sometimes the way may be difficult, but he never promised it would be easy. Life is a test and our agency allows us the choice to decide which way, in varying degrees, to go. We can choose to be angry and bitter about our situation and seek justice, or we can look at our blessings, which are many, and keep our heads held high.

Now, I could end this book right here because this story is the main reason I started writing in the first place, but I have a few more things I really need to say. Things that I feel are so important that I suggest you keep reading to the end.

Chapter 18

Mom Brennan

Mom Brennan moved to Ivins about 4 years before she died. She couldn't believe that she would get a raise when she put in for a transfer to St. George. She would have moved sooner had she known. Silly Mary! The community and staff at DRMC all fell for Mom B. Hiking every day; walking Sam, her big sheepdog; being around the grandkids... life was good... for a while. Mary was a temple going nut. She had 3000 names to do temple work for and was always falling asleep while visiting us. *She worked three 13 hour shifts straight and then spent her days off in the temple.* She started to have some back pain, more than normal, and after some X-rays found that her vertebrae in her back had collapsed into each other. She had a severe case of bone cancer, originating from some breast lumps. Chemo & radiation therapy were on order.

The 15 chapters it would take to go through the details of chemo and radiation would be too dark to go into. Suffice it to say, I was her 24-hour caretaker. In that short 3-month span, I lost my job because I had to keep leaving to help her. My poor family, but I could not leave her side. The only way they would see me during that time was to visit my mom, where I usually was. I always seemed to know exactly what she needed when it was time for it and she was always giving me hugs of gratitude. Mom's friend, Ellie, came and stayed for two weeks. She's a friend from back in Springfield. What a breath of fresh air she was! I didn't even know what to do with myself with that time off, except maybe think about getting a job… but I mostly slept.

There was a time when mom was at the Red Cliffs Care Center and was all hooked up to her morphine pump and fluids and my brother Carl and I kidnapped her! The attendant saw that we were taking her and figured there was nothing he could do about it, so he helped us with the morphine pump, to make it more portable. It was nice that he helped us, as we were going to take her either way. She was missing her home and fresh air and needed a break. It was a beautiful day with the birds singing, and we were all listening to the noises of the neighborhood, while she was lazily feeling the breeze on the front porch. Some kids down the street were just being kids, laughing and playing loudly, when my brother Carl yelled, "Shut up! My mom's tryin' ta get some rest!" It was so abrupt, he scared us both to laughing! The peaceful scene, followed by hearty laughter with those I love, will remain precious in my memory. There were hard times to come, but many of them held tender memories.

There was one night at the hospital when the only comfort she could find was when I wrapped her sheet behind her and held both ends of it, cradling her so she could lean back into an upright position. That was the only comfort from pain she could get. I held the sheet in place all night long. My knuckles were white from lack of blood. It got very painful for me, but I kept looking at how peaceful she was sleeping and could not let go. Mom was in out of the hospital in her final days. Many of our tender memories with her were when she was able to come home. She loved to sleep in her own bed with her cat, and the grandchildren were able to visit every day.

While my kids were saying they're good nights to their grandma, each one would take a turn giving her a kiss on the forehead and getting a hug. One night, I noticed the boy that went with us to California earlier that summer was in line to say goodnight to my mom and when he kissed her forehead and she hugged him back I knew right then and there that young man was going to be my son-in-law! I just knew he would be part of our family, and that came out of nowhere! *That actually came out of Heaven! In Heavenly Father's playground there's a seesaw and when we're on it, and we're down, he's on the other side and it's up and there's a blessing attached to that. So, as soon as you come out of your depression, you'll catch the vision of what Father's giving you. Or if you're just going to sit there and have a pity party and cry, you won't notice the hands that are reaching down to pick you up. So just always remember "every low has its opposite."*

I didn't know it at the time, but Tiffany had been instructed by her grandma how to tell who's a keeper and which ones to get rid of. Tiff really liked this boy, Ryan, a lot but he never flattered her the way the other guys did, and, at the time, she thought this was very important; probably because of how I always taught the girls they are priceless. They are Heavenly Father's princesses here on earth for a short time. When you go back to Heaven, you enter back into royalty. One particular day, she had pushed him so far away without communicating to anyone why. What teenage girl wants to admit that they need more compliments? That would seem pretty shallow.

She went to spend some time with Grandma Mary, as Grandma was not doing very well. Her time on earth was getting very short and she was rarely awake anymore and could hardly speak. As Tiff was kissing her goodnight, Grandma reached out and grabbed her hand as tight as she could in her weakened state, and Tiff could tell that she had some serious business. She proceeded to tell her that that boy, Ryan, was very special and gave the most amazing blessings and prayers. She told Tiff that she would marry that boy. She told her exactly what she needed to hear. She told her how "any guy can tell you what you want to hear, but it takes a real man to actually show he is sincere". Then she told her a story about men.

She said, "Your grandfather always told me how beautiful I was! But he also told his girlfriend, the lady who lived next-door, and lots of other women how gorgeous they were too. It's not in what they say; it's how they treat you. Ryan is a keeper! You take the things he does for you and hold them as a thousand words, because a true genuine guy like that is hard to find. You hold onto that young man!" Tiff was shocked to hear the answer to something that no one even knew she was thinking about. She kept this story to herself for years, until she was mature enough to understand the depth of how amazing that answer was. Heavenly Father knows our thoughts and our needs, even when we don't realize it.

It was just a couple days after mom's funeral that Tiffany approached me with "I'm in love and I would like to get married." That hit me like a brick to the back of my head. I was standing there spinning in my thoughts about how depressed and dark everything seemed, now the total opposite? I even remember thinking, I guess life goes on…

"Sure Tiff. I mean, do you know that this is the right guy? Of course, I know he is, but I want your thoughts about him. Will you ask Heavenly Father his opinion too?"

"Yes, I will", she said.

But you see, thinking back to just a few days before, Heavenly Father knew this question was going to come up and he told me when Ryan said good night to mom Brennan, that he belonged in our family. I knew! I did not even have to fast and pray to find out and ask questions. Father already revealed it to me. When one door closes, another one opens. I quickly had to step through that open door of planning a wedding!

Why do Mormon women stop having babies at 35? Because 36 babies are far too many!

Paul Joseph Brennan

Chapter 19

My Gulfport Miracle

When our son, Joseph, was 15 years old, he decided he wanted to help the people that were affected by the Hurricane Katrina, which was so devastating to so many. He chose to do his Eagle Scout project by filling a semi with donations of Walmart so generously agreed to donate a tractor-trailer and said they would donate a driver and cover those expenses if it was filled with donations. Joseph worked alongside a lady that was already working on donations as well, and within less than a week they had a tractor-trailer full of things like clothing, diapers, baby items, blankets, 72-hour kits in buckets, food, etc. The response was over whelming! It was a huge job for a 15-year old! He also received some cash donations. He was able to give most of the cash immediately, but it was very difficult to decide where to best donate the remainder of the cash.

It was getting very close to Christmas and there was still $1800.00 cash left in the account. Joey wanted to make sure that someone received it before Christmas. We talked to a friend who was from that area and he found someone that we felt really needed the money the most. She was a 70 plus year-old mother/grandmother that had lost her home three times to hurricanes and a fire. She was struggling to get her home rebuilt this time, due to the large amount of damage. The plan was set to have her grown children give the money to her in a Christmas card on Christmas Eve. This was to be a surprise to her. It worked out wonderfully, as expected. She was very surprised and humbled. We all felt very happy that the money went to someone who was so thankful and deserving. We wished we could have met her, but there was not enough money for that.

Not long after this, I was working in the devastated Gulfport area, trying to help with clean up and rebuilding. I saw so many in need and wished we had much more money to give. I was working long days and weeks away from my family and it was quite depressing seeing all the devastation. On a Sunday in January, I was getting ready for my day and knew I wanted to attend a church service somewhere. So, I said a prayer that I could find a chapel and refill my much-needed reservoir with something that would lift my spirit so I could go on for the next week. I asked Heavenly Father to bless me with something to help me. I used my modern day "Liahona", my cell phone, to locate a chapel that would hopefully have a meeting beginning at 9:00 am. It was a pretty crowded chapel, but I found a spot front and center when I arrived. I ended up in the middle of a big row filled with people on both sides. I knew no one. I was a little claustrophobic and wishing I was on the end of a row.

That Sunday ended up being Fast and Testimony meeting for some reason, even though it wasn't the first Sunday of the month. *This is where anyone in the congregation can go up and share their testimony at the pulpit.* Because of the things that everyone there had been through, and were still going through, the meeting went over time. The spirit was very strong, but I was still feeling claustrophobic. I would have gotten up and left, but I didn't want to disrupt everyone trying to get out past them. Then an older adorable sister got up to bear her testimony. She started speaking about how she was blessed with a miracle that Christmas. How there was a young man from

Utah that had cared enough to help an old lady so far away. She said she had wanted to thank him and had written him a letter, but couldn't get his address to send it. So, she decided to publicly thank him there instead. She wanted to say his name out loud, even though she knew no one knew him.

When she said the name "Joseph Brennan" from Utah, the tears started falling so hard, I almost let out a loud cry! I couldn't believe my ears! This sweet lady was talking about my son! I was so happy that I couldn't contain myself. I'm sure all the people around me were wondering what my problem was… Here I am, a stranger to them all and I'm bawling my head off and making lots of strange noises trying to keep it all in! She said she wished she could get the letter to him, but this was the only thing she knew to do. She humbly thanked Heavenly Father for young men in the church who cared enough to help people they didn't even know. Then she sat down.

I wanted to stay there and talk to her after the meeting and tell her who I was, but God obviously wanted the congregation to be blessed with this miracle as well. I could not sit there, as hard as I tried. I went to the pulpit and introduced myself. I explained how I had randomly picked that time and place. I told that sweet lady that I could and would love to deliver that letter to that boy because I was his father! There were no dry eyes in the congregation! Was it a coincidence that I happened to be there? Or was it an "ordinary miracle?" I'd say it was no coincidence and no *"ordinary"* miracle. It was a gift from God to both her and I that wonderful Sabbath day! Miracles are all around us! All we need to do is believe, and then ask! And of course, live the kind of life that, when Heavenly Father wants to bless us, we'll take notice and not just brush it off as a mere coincidence. I went through the next week with my spirit full and my attitude ready for whatever came!

Just a note… Fast and Testimony Meeting in the Mormon Church is usually the first Sunday of each month. It is a day that everyone who chooses to can fast for up to 24 hours and donate the money that would be spent on food to the church to help others locally that may need help financially.

Chapter 20

Jessica's Story

When our daughter Jessica was 19 years old, she came to us and told us that she was in love and wanted to get married. She was dating a young man that seemed like a great guy. He had served a mission and seemed to really love our daughter. Still, this was kind of a surprise because this was the daughter that, shortly before that, wanted no part of settling down or getting married young. She wanted to travel and see the world first. She had lots of aspirations. So, when we saw things were changing, I, as her father, had to start getting serious. I needed to ask God if this young man was right for her. Of course, I told her that she also needed to make sure that God was good with her decision. One problem... I didn't get the answer she was hoping for.

I didn't have a good feeling that this young man was right for her. I let her know of my inspiration, but what 19-year old wants to listen to her dad when she's in love? So, I gave her my blessing, even though it didn't feel right. There was no outward reason to be concerned, just a feeling when I prayed about it. Well, another wedding was planned and the happy couple settled in to married life. Jessica opened a small salon and life seemed good for them. To make a long eight years not seem so long, their marriage ended after many difficult times. It was a tough eight years for Jessica. She felt early on that it wasn't going to last forever, so she had focused on her career instead of bringing any babies into the marriage. Most people that knew her, figured she was just a career girl and didn't want kids.

When her marriage ended, she was very lost. Her dream of her "forever" marriage was gone! She had tried to do everything right, so why did this happen… She was really struggling and was bitter. She kind of just shut off emotionally. She'd been through a lot. We just loved her and gave her time and many, many prayers. She is a strong girl, but she just seemed to stay on that dark road of depression and bitterness. Sometimes, as parents, as hard as we try, we can't fix our children's problems they go through in life. They have to experience things for themselves. Sometimes the only thing we can do is pray… and pray hard! Some parents go through years and years of sadness and sorrow with their children. Jessica was and is a princess, but she didn't feel like one and certainly hadn't been treated like one for a while by her husband.

She lost hope that there was someone amazing out there for her and that true happiness could be hers. But God had a miracle in store for her too. Not long after this, Jessica met the man of her dreams, "Prince Andrew." He somehow knew just what she needed to hear to remind her that she was a princess and that she had worth. She knew what she needed to do to get back on track. *I'm pretty sure we prayed him into her life! Just sayin'…* She made a 180-degree turn around and it didn't take long for her to fall in love again. Who could blame her? She had met her prince!

Andrew had recently been through his own trials and was also hurting from a recent divorce. It's interesting to look back and see how the trials that Jess went through in her first marriage made her who she is today and put her in the perfect position to find Andrew. The timing was so perfect! Heavenly Father blesses us though our trials. He knows what we need and when we need it. He didn't take away her pain as she was hurting, but he helped her through it and helped her get back on track in her life. Never give up no matter how bad it seems. Hang in there and keep believing! Listen to God, instead of getting angry at how your life is. Going through trials is part of this earth life. Stuff is going to hurt! Life is going to be messy! Just know that God won't give up on you! He knows you better than anyone and loves you unconditionally.

Jessica now has an amazing little family with two of the cutest little guys on the planet... well not so little as they are very tall for their ages. They get that from their dad who is 6'5". Who knew that she wasn't just a career girl after all? Parents... never give up! Keep on praying for your children no matter what! Never stop! They are worth it and those prayers are heard, even if you feel like nothing is changing or getting better. I know that the prayers my mom prayed meant something and made a difference in my life. Heavenly Father knows how much we love our children. He loves them as well and he can see from his vantage point much better than us what they need. He also gives them agency to make their own decisions. He loves them unconditionally and so must we. He sees their full potential, who they really are and who they can become.

I think a huge part of good parenting is patience and understanding, as well as respect. We've always respected our children, even when they were small. In return, they have always respected us as parents and the mutual relationship we share is amazing. We have always been told that we have a very close family and that it is unusual these days. Our children have always been more important to us than anything else. They know that and feel that. Now, our grandchildren are the living proof that we've done something right. They are amazing people with so much to give to the world. And the world needs great people! Life has given back so much more than it has taken, but it's all in your attitude! Life is what you make of it and I'm so glad I'm still here to make as much of it as I can in the time I have left.

Chapter 21

The Rest of the Story

"When I was a child, I spake as a child, I understood as a child, I thought as a child: but when I became a man, I put away childish things" (1 Corinthians 13:11).

The apostle Paul, of the New Testament, had an interesting life. He was a Roman citizen and had all the rights, privileges and authority that went with that. He had freedom to move about, crossing borders without question. This helped him in his quest seeking out Christians and putting them to death. I picture him with a fearless, resolute will of an independent nature that you would not want to cross, or have him seek *you* out! Joseph, who's experiences are chronicled in Genesis in the Old Testament, also had an interesting life. Very sad and challenging at times, but interesting. His dad was very wealthy and Joseph had an army of brothers. He should have been able to feel protected and yet his own brothers wanted to kill him. They eventually sold him into slavery.

Joseph was such a humble servant of God that he never played the hand of "My dad's very powerful, so if I were you I would think twice about taking me. He's got enough authority and money to hire people like the apostle Paul to come find me and put to death anybody who dares take me." Joseph was a resilient youth. I think he enjoyed the travel and meeting new people, as he was highly educated from his father's knee in all things. He knew how to read and write in his Hebrew tongue, and learned much of the Torah and local government policies. It's no wonder that, when he was placed in any position, even as a prisoner, he knew what the circumstance required, and he was willing to do it He was always willing to help, even in a servant capacity. More than anything, I think, he had implicit faith that God would oversee his every move.

When he was exposed to the dreams of the servant and the cook, God opened his mind and revealed to him the interpretation. Being trained from the cradle, being prepared for his mission, it was easy for him to rise to the top. Especially, when it came time to feed the nations and he became second only to the Pharaoh in the Egyptian government. More interesting to me, though, was the fact that in his time, living amongst the Egyptians, he learned their language, their laws and their religious beliefs. He was so well documented in their lifestyle that it was easy for him to speak through an interpreter when his brother showed up to purchase food. I love thinking about these stories and how God has a hand in all our lives. He is watching over us and will guide us and help us, if we only have faith in him. He won't take away a person's agency, but he can help us to make the most of any situation we find ourselves in.

The stories in the Holy Bible are so inspiring to me, but an even more inspiring and amazing story is one that happened much later. The story of a 14-year old boy, also named Joseph, that had a burning question only God could answer. He knew that God would answer his prayer because of how he felt when he read James 1:5. When Heavenly Father answered his prayer, it was only the beginning of the restoration of all things prophesied. Several years later, more of the restoration was given to the boy prophet, specifically involving his ancestry who escaped the Babylonian overthrow. They flourished across this whole nation, having prophets that lived and prophesied among them. All that history, spanning 1000 years, was recorded upon plates and handed down from generation to generation until finally from father to son, Mormon to Moroni, with their last inspired words. Their final testimony in Christ closed the events of their history. Opening this dispensation, the Angel Moroni gave Joseph Smith, the boy Prophet, this record from his own hand.

God the Father and his Son, Jesus Christ, appeared to Joseph as glorified individuals in the form of men. God introduced his son to Joseph, calling Joseph by name. Because of God's mercy for us, the true and everlasting Gospel has been restored and sacred temples of the Lord have been erected to do his work. There are no more sacred places on earth than his holy temples, where covenants and authority are bestowed upon man from God! This is the only difference between Latter-Day Saints and all other Christians. We both believe in the same God. It's through his Holy of Holy's that all mankind can and will be sealed to each other and, more importantly, to him!

If I were to have stayed Catholic, I would still be of the belief that my beautiful twin daughters, who died after only living one day, because they did not have the opportunity to be baptized before they died, would be in purgatory forever! I now know, through living prophets, that little children are celestial heirs and are glorified and perfected in their innocence without sin. They are pure! Just as much as those that are unable to comprehend sin. They are also heirs to the Kingdom of God. And it's through these holy temples that all our families can be linked together forever. From our ancestral dead, who's work can be done by proxy, to the tiniest new baby born. We are all linked together! This is God's plan for all mankind. Even with this, every individual still has his or her agency to choose to accept it or reject it.

Now, I know about history and I know about Constantine and his passion for power. I also know of the eminent death Christians faced; yet, they faced it fearlessly! He coveted that bravado and eventually became a Christian. It was his becoming a Christian that derailed all the priests and teachers, evangelists and deacons that were set up by the apostle Paul. The apostle who we all know put a lot of Christians to death before his own conversion. Christ's Apostles were also driven from pillar to post and slaughtered, so that Constantine could direct the affairs of his newfound fearless army. The true church of Christ was dissected; it was pulverized and counterfeited. The sacred power of Christ was taken away and replaced with man's wisdom. Thus, the dark ages...

It was through the dark ages that the great reformers evolved. They evolved because they biblically knew and understood that there would be a refreshing of all things, from the holy prophets. As decades passed, the followers of those reformers lost their vision of the prophecy and stood resolute, each in their own faith. Somewhere in the midst of time, from then to now, their progenitors became stalwart believers that they each had the ultimate gift from God, the truth, and they splintered off from each other. That's why we have thousands of different Christian denominations. With all of them believing in the Bible so differently, is it any wonder that a 14-year old boy named Joseph Smith was confused as to which church to join? When he left the grove the day he had witnessed two holy personages, he had received his answer from Heavenly Father to join none of the churches. He was told, "...they draw near me with their lips, but their hearts are far from me..." (Joseph Smith – History 1:19).

Several years later, Joseph was visited by more angelic messengers who bestowed upon him God's authority to reorganize his Kingdom on earth. A very important part of this was the authority to baptize in his name, as well as perform other sacred ordinances in the temples. One of the important ordinances in the temple is the sealing ordinance linking families from the beginning of time to forever. This most important work has to be done by those given authority from God. Through your efforts and mine, we can help our ancestral dead gain those most important ordinances to seal them up to come forth in the morning of the first resurrection, as they so deserve. As my brother Bobby wanted.

Remember when an 11-year-old boy was being asked by his mother whom he wanted to live with, his mother or his father? My answer had been that I wanted to live with both of them and my mother had left the room, shaking her head, knowing that was impossible and I was too young and immature to understand the fact that they could not get along. Many years later, having a family of my own, my wife and I went to the St. George Temple and knelt across the holy altar from each other. I, acting as proxy for my dad, and my wife Karen, acting as proxy for my mom, sealed them together for time and all eternity! But we didn't stop there... We then changed places and I was able to represent my brother Bobby. I sealed him to our parents, as well. This was the beginning of the realization of my childhood dream. To be with *both* my parents!

While writing this book, my sister passed away, so she's next on the list. Although, I might make her wait a little extra time for all the stuff she put me through! No, not really. I am excited to have her sealed to our family. With all my heart, I know this is a true never-ending story! There's not a more perfect happily-ever after story. You can't top this! To my Christian friends, I love you! I know that Jesus loves you! That's why he made us friends. He trusts in my personality disorder to open my big mouth and testify to you what the good news is! God's church has been restored. The angel spoken of in Revelations has already flown! I know his name. It's Moroni.

> *"And I saw another angel fly in the midst of heaven, having the everlasting gospel to preach unto them that dwell on the earth, and to every nation, and kindred, and tongue, and people…"* *(Revelations 14:6).*

His hand was the last to engrave in that sacred record his last will and testament. He put a promise in the book that stands even today.

> *"Behold, I would exhort you that when ye shall read these things, if it be wisdom in God that ye should read them, that ye would remember how merciful the Lord hath been unto the children of men, from the creation of Adam even down until the time that ye shall receive these things, and ponder it in your hearts.*

> *"And when ye shall receive these things, I would exhort you that ye would ask God, the Eternal Father, in the name of Christ, if these things are not true; and if ye shall ask with a sincere heart, with real intent, having faith in Christ, he will manifest the truth of it unto you, by the power of the Holy Ghost.*

> *"And by the power of the Holy Ghost ye may know the truth of all things"* *(Moroni 10:3-5).*

The Holy Ghost is the witness to and bearer of all truth. He is the eternal guiding compass, the Liahona to heaven, the Celestial GPS (Gods Prophetic Sonar). An optimum gift from tender merciful heavenly parents to me and to you! I promise you that, if you read the Book of Mormon, it will change your life. It will either bring you closer to understanding why you're on planet earth or you might just get angry and throw this book down and call it trash and that spirit will be part of you until you decide to look for the truth. Because of a loving Father in Heaven, the choice is yours!

Paul Joseph Brennan

Chapter 22

Reflections

Now that you've been a ride along on my journey of life, looking over my shoulder and picking up pieces of Paul along the way... my aspirations for you my friends would be for you to have been catching your own vision reading between the lines. I hope that you begin to feel like the greatest treasure on earth that you really are. I know this, because I have been to the other side and back. I am a living testament to this. Being buried is inevitably one thing that we all will have in common at some point. Totally uncommon though, never heard of before in my research, is being buried under 12 feet of earth and coming back out to talk about it.

Earnest prayers at life's most trying moments never fall on deaf ears! As the sparrow falls to the earth, seemingly unnoticed, the infinite wisdom of a divine creator knows how many barbicels are in each feather. **Each one of us has, at least, the potential of a sparrow.** Know this... Through the all-seeing eyes of loving, heavenly parents, everything about you and about me is known and counted! I testify to you and to my beloved family, we are of most precious worth to those, our heavenly parents. They created each of us, from whence we came and the earth we now stand on and all the everyday beauties that surround us. Not only their eyes perceive our next and every move, but also the eyes of our noble ancestor's rally and cheer us on in hopes that we keep our precious birthright.

"...for they that be with us are more than they that be with them" (2 Kings 6:16).

They who stand with us are greater than they who stand against us. To this I am certain. I've seen the enemy, face to face! Make no mistake, you and I are no match to this ruler of darkness in high places. But the Lord is! The fact is, your birthright may have already been taken from you. That's how cunning the father of all lies is! Don't kid yourself into thinking you're different and can outsmart an entity that has never forgotten who we all are. He, rest assured, being there from our beginnings, at our birth, has patiently been waiting and silent note taking on what moves us to be naughty, not nice. So, you'd better watch out! Yeah, just like Santa, only extremely well read! Free agency is a gift. Now don't get me wrong, I am not saying he is going to win. This is why... Divine Intervention.

We've all been promised there will never be temptation beyond our ability. There will always be a safe haven and a way out! As soon as you decide in your soul to overcome evil, divine intervention will deliver you from what could have potentially destroyed you. You, through the atoning blood of Christ, can win back your birthright. But only through him! I know that God lives and speaks through a living prophet today. I also know that our value is far greater than anything this planet has to offer, because the yardstick that I measure with is from eternity. All of us have passed through the veil to get here and all of us will pass through again when we die and are buried. Very few of us are fortunate enough to traverse the veil and come back.

So important is personal time for scripture study! And while listening to the voice reading the words, ponder those words in your mind for inspiration. Write those thoughts, desires and ideas down. This is Heavenly Father's way of communicating to you the way you need to be or what you should do to bring about change, moving towards the good, repenting of the bad.

"There is no passion to be found playing small - in settling for a life that is less than the one you are capable of living."

– Nelson Mandela

I love to think BIG! I don't want you to confuse thinking big with being egotistical or prideful. I just enjoy being the underdog against insurmountable mountains and only God could be acknowledged for my victories! Divine intervention has come into play many times in my life and I totally believe that we can change our stars! By strict obedience to the commandments laid before us and listening to a living prophet, and being diligent in all things required of us. Ask and you shall receive. Knock and it shall be opened. Pray and multiple tons of dirt will be removed, and you will live the life you promised yourself, your children and your ancestors you would live. You will then be encircled about by your faithful loved ones, when it *is* your time to return home. But most importantly, a kind, loving Heavenly Father will enshroud you with his love when he greets you in that heavenly mansion above.

"Great it is to believe the dream, when we stand in youth by the starry stream. But a greater thing it is to fight life through and say at the end the dream was true!"

– Edward Markham

Paul Joseph Brennan

Author's Notes

"Under pressure" viewed in my mind…

A WWII Navy Submarine weakened by depth chargers and having to lay silent at the bottom of the ocean floor until the enemy seeking to destroy it flees towards a greater design. The sub slips deeper into the fathoms of the ocean until the external pipes burst into imploding doom. Steam, giving way, blowing out the valves. Men say their final salute to each other, then turn inward in a selfless pause of gratitude, having no regrets to have lived a hero's life. Now, kissing the memory of loved ones safe at home, amid a plight to praise God and end this fight…

The engines suddenly kick in and, in an upward thrust, leave the floor of the ocean to continue on and leave behind the dark abyss to once again thrive, twice blessed for another chance to live a nobler life. Not only the ship, but the precious cargo, as well.

We are all under pressure in different ways, at different times in our lives. So many that cause us to make choices both big and small, leaving room for life changing experiences that we may not even realize are there. Choice is a gift that we have been given in this life. Being under pressure can cause us to look to God for help and guidance so that, hopefully, we will live the life we were meant to live. After all, a piece of coal with the right pressure, cut and polished, will become a priceless diamond. It is my hope that you will become the brilliant diamond you were meant to be. An example to others of what we all can become!

ABOUT AUTHOR

Paul Joseph Brennan was born in the Boston Children's Hospital. He was one of five children. His early childhood memories were happy, even though his family had some troubles. Then the trials became such that he quit school and left home at the age of fourteen.

His education consisted mostly from the school of hard knocks, a tough taskmaster. His journey through his trials was difficult, but he is grateful that he was able to survive and find joy in his life.

Paul's wife and family are his greatest treasure. Their married children and grandchildren live near them in Southern Utah. They now even have some great grandkids! But Papa Paul has been heard to say, "we're not just great grandparents, we're *awesome* grandparents!" Some of their grandkids love to perform and have entertained people all over the country. They've even been on a few television shows. But "Nana" and "Papa" will always be their biggest fans! Check them out on Youtube at McDonald Family Adventures.

For updates on Paul Joseph Brennan and his family's journey go to *www.pauljosephbrennan.com*

ACKNOWLEDGEMENTS

We have been led to many wonderful friends in this journey. Some old friends, some new. Thanks to Pat Canning for taking on the most difficult job of the first edit. She had barely met us when she offered to read and edit the first manuscript. What a job that must have been! She has become a cherished friend.

Then we found our friends from the past, the Clarke family. What a blessing they have been! George and Linda and their family have taken us from not knowing where to go from where we were, to getting this book to a finished masterpiece. You may find Linda's website at lindaweaverclarke.com.

Their daughter, Diana Clarke Broadhead, did a second and third edit. She put her whole heart into this work. (Thanks to her family for allowing her the time to do this work). Her sister, Serena Clarke did all the work to make the cover. She does amazing work. Her website can be found at serenaclarke.wordpress.com. They have had all the answers we needed and we wouldn't be where we are today without this wonderful family.

Thanks to a kind Heavenly Father for allowing me to stick around long enough to have all these experiences and live through them to find the joy this life has to offer. You may find Him at lds.org.

Thanks to Jesse Clyde Sumsion for helping to put me on a path to climb out of the darkness of my past. Thanks to Leon

Stubbs for his inspiration to say the right words to put me back on that path a few years later. Thanks to Admiral C. Monroe Hart for having the inspiration to tell me his story that saved my life years later.

Thanks to all the friends that were there to help me along my journey, to get to where I am today. There are many. Too many to mention, but you know who you are and the part you have played in my life. There's a poem that I love. It says, "Make new friends, but keep the old. One is silver, the other gold." (Leaves of Gold)

Thanks to my family for putting up with my kind of crazy that came from a past like mine. And even though my mom has graduated planet earth, thanks Mom for never giving up on me and always seeing the good in me. Thanks for being willing to change your life when you saw a better way. You are my hero.

To my girlfriend KC (Karen Campbell), whom I "sold on" marrying me. I Love You, KC! Now impossible as it is to say in brief, I am so grateful for the endless, charitable, and forever faithful efforts you are cheerfully guilty of. Thank you, my amazingly strong and beautiful wife, Karen. You have stayed by my side for all of these years and suffered just like our wonderful children did. All of us, being dragged through stuff: good and bad! I'm convinced my family should write their own book on their perspectives of our family's journeys.

This woman has been my biggest support, cheerleader, and word-fixer. My thoughts often come after a conversation with her. When my thoughts are hard to get out in a manner that others can appreciate, she edits them into something understandable, and on occasion has stopped me with a ten count.

This book would not have been possible without her unconditional love for me and constant patience and support. She is the "behind the scenes" director, who makes our lives flow so beautifully. This too is her story, but from my perspective. I would love for her to write her thoughts of this miraculous journey, as I'm sure we would all enjoy. She is an inspired poet and eloquent writer.

My mom picked Karen out for me. Read the book! She knew I would need an angel to make it through this life. Thanks, mom! She is my most treasured gift.

And thank you Karen for carin'!

BIBLIOGRAPHY

Leaves of Gold: An Anthology of Memorable Phrases, Inspirational Verse and Prose by Clyde Frances Lytle (Editor); The Coslett Publishing Co., January 1, 1948

The Holy Bible, Authorized King James Version; Published by The Church of Jesus Christ of Latter-Day Saints, Copyright 1979

The Book of Mormon, Another Testament of Jesus Christ translated by Joseph Smith, Jr.; Published by the Church of Jesus Christ of Latter-Day Saints, 1989 (First edition published in 1830)

Made in USA - Kendallville, IN
20238_9781981218882
09.25.2022 1244